W9-CCD-176

INHERIT THE WIND

BY
JEROME LAWRENCE
AND **ROBERT E. LEE**

★

★

DRAMATISTS
PLAY SERVICE
INC.

INHERIT THE WIND
Copyright © 2000 (Revised), Jerome Lawrence and Janet Waldo Lee,
Trustee of the Robert E. Lee and Janet Waldo Lee Living Trust
Copyright © 1986, Jerome Lawrence and Robert E. Lee (Two-Act Version)
Copyright © Renewed 1979, 1983, 1986, 1991,
Jerome Lawrence and Robert E. Lee
Copyright © 1958, 1963 (Revised), Jerome Lawrence and Robert E. Lee
Copyright © 1951, 1955, Jerome Lawrence and Robert E. Lee

All Rights Reserved

SPECIAL NOTE

AUTHORS' NOTE

INHERIT THE WIND is not history. The events which took place in Dayton, Tennessee, during the scorching July of 1925 are clearly the genesis of this play. It has, however, an exodus entirely its own.

Only a handful of phrases have been taken from the actual transcript of the famous Scopes trial. Some of the characters of the play are related to the colorful figures in that battle of giants; but they have life and language of their own — and, therefore, names of their own.

The greatest reporters and historians of the century have written millions of words about the "Monkey Trial." We are indebted to them for their brilliant reportage. And we are grateful to the late Arthur Garfield Hays, who recounted to us much of the unwritten vividness of the Dayton adventure from his own memory and experience.

The collision of Bryan and Darrow at Dayton was dramatic, but it was not a drama. Moreover, the issues of their conflict have acquired new dimensions and meaning in the years since they clashed at the Rhea County Courthouse. So INHERIT THE WIND does not pretend to be journalism. It is theatre. It is not 1925. The stage directions set the time as "Not too long ago." It might have been yesterday. It could be tomorrow.

Jerome Lawrence
Robert E. Lee

INHERIT THE WIND was presented on Broadway by Herman Shumlin, in association with Margo Jones, at the National Theatre, New York City, April 21, 1955, with the following cast:

RACHEL BROWN .... Bethel Leslie
MEEKER .... Robert P. Lieb
BERTRAM CATES .... Karl Light
MR. GOODFELLOW .... Salem Ludwig
MRS. KREBS .... Sarah Floyd
REV. JEREMIAH BROWN .... Staats Cotsworth
CORKIN .... Fred Herrick
BOLLINGER .... Donald Elson
PLATT .... Fred Miller
MR. BANNISTER .... Charles Thompson
MELINDA .... Mary Kevin Kelly
HOWARD .... Eric Berne
MRS. LOOMIS .... Rita Newton
HOT DOG MAN .... Howard Caine
MRS. McLAIN .... Margherita Sargent
MRS. BLAIR .... Ruth Newton
ELIJAH .... Charles Brin
E.K. HORNBECK .... Tony Randall
HURDY GURDY MAN .... Harry Shaw
TIMMY .... Jack Banning
MAYOR .... James Maloney
MATTHEW HARRISON BRADY .... Ed Begley
MRS. BRADY .... Muriel Kirkland
TOM DAVENPORT .... William Darrid
HENRY DRUMMOND .... Paul Muni
JUDGE .... Louis Hector
DUNLAP .... Fred Miller
SILLERS .... Fred Herrick
REUTERS MAN .... Edmund Williams
HARRY Y. ESTERBROOK .... Perry Fiske

SCIENTISTS, TOWNSPEOPLE, HAWKERS, REPORTERS, JURORS, SPECTATORS played by: Lou Adelman, Joseph Brownstone, Clifford Carpenter, Michael Constantine, Michael

Del Medico, James Greene, Ruth Hope, Sally Jessup, Julie Knox, Patricia Larson, Michael Lewin, Evelyn Mando, Sarah Meade, Gian Pace, Richard Poston, Jack Riano, Gordon Russell, Carroll Saint, Robert Shannon, Maurice Shrog.

Directed by Herman Shumlin
Settings by Peter Larkin
Lighting by Feder
Costumes by Ruth Morley
Assistant Director: Terese Hayden

INHERIT THE WIND was first presented at the Dallas Theatre '55 on January 10, 1955. The cast included Edward Cullen, J. Frank Lucas, James Field, Louise Latham, Harry Bergman, Michael Dolan, Kathleen Phelan, Gilbert Milton, Edwin Whitner, Joe Walker, Dolores Walker, John Maddox, Sadie French, Sam Brunstein, Tommy Wright, Joe Parker, Joan Breymer, Harriet Slaughter, Eddie Gale, Morgan Wilson, Charlie West and Fred Hoskins. Margo Jones directed.

Melvyn Douglas replaced Paul Muni as Drummond on Broadway, then on Muni's return launched a year-long tour throughout the United States and Canada. INHERIT THE WIND has been translated and produced in 34 languages, including Spanish, Hebrew, German, Russian, Irdu, Serbo-Croatian, and many others.

The film version, directed by Stanley Kramer, starred Spencer Tracy, Fredric March, Gene Kelly.

A 1996 Broadway revival starred George C. Scott and Charles Durning.

A 1999 movie for television, directed by Daniel Petrie Sr., starred George C. Scott and Jack Lemmon.

"He that troubleth his own house
Shall inherit the wind."

Proverbs 11:29

PLACE

A small town.

TIME

Summer. Not too long ago.

INHERIT THE WIND

ACT ONE

Scene 1

In and around the Hillsboro Courthouse. The foreground is the actual courtroom, with jury box, judge's bench and a scattering of trial-scarred chairs and counsel tables. The back wall of the courtroom is non-existent. On a raked level above it is the courthouse square, the Main Street and the converging streets of the town. This is not so much a literal view of Hillsboro as it is an impression of a sleepy, obscure country town about to be vigorously awakened.

It is important to the concept of the play that the town is visible always, looming there, as much on trial as the individual defendant. The crowd is equally important throughout, so that the court becomes an arena, with active spectators on all sides of it. It is an hour after dawn on a July day that promises to be a scorcher. Howard, a boy of thirteen, wanders onto the courthouse lawn. He is barefoot, wearing a pair of his pa's cut-down overalls. He carries an improvised fishing pole and a tin can. He studies the ground carefully, searching for something. A young girl's voice calls from offstage.

MELINDA. *(Calling sweetly.)* How-ard...! *(Howard, annoyed, turns and looks toward the voice. Melinda, a healthy, pigtailed girl of twelve, skips on.)* Hello, Howard. *(Howard is disinterested, continues to search the ground.)*

HOWARD. 'Lo, Melinda.

MELINDA. *(Making conversation.)* I think it's gonna be hotter'n yesterday. That rain last night didn't do much good.

HOWARD. *(Professionally.)* It brought up the worms. *(Suddenly he spots one in the lawn. Swiftly he grabs for it, and holds it up proudly.)* Lookit this fat one! *(He chases her.)*

MELINDA. *(Shivering.)* How can you touch 'em? It makes me all goose-bumpy! *(Howard dangles it in front of her face. She backs away, shuddering.)*

HOWARD. What're yuh skeered of? *You* was a worm once!

MELINDA. *(Shocked.)* I wasn't neither!

HOWARD. You was so! When the whole world was covered with water, there was nuthin' but worms and blobs of jelly. And you and your whole family was worms!

MELINDA. We was not!

HOWARD. Blobs of jelly, then.

MELINDA. Howard Blair, that's sinful talk! I'm gonna tell my Pa and he'll make you wash your mouth out with soap!

HOWARD. Ahhh, your old man's a monkey! *(Melinda gasps. She turns indignantly and runs off. Howard shrugs in the manner of a man-of-the-world.)* 'Bye, Lindy. *(Rachel enters. She is 22, pretty, but not beautiful. She wears a cotton summer dress. She carries a small composition paper suitcase. There is a tense, distraught air about her. She may have been crying. She looks about nervously, as if she doesn't want to be seen. When she sees Howard, she hesitates, then she scurries downstage into the courthouse area in the hope that the boy will not notice her. But he does see Rachel, and watchers her with puzzled curiosity. Then as he exits he addresses the worm, dangling it in the air.)* What do you wanta be when you grow up? *(He goes off. Rachel stands uncertainly in the courthouse area. Unsure, she looks about.)*

RACHEL. *(Tentatively, calling.)* Mr. Meeker...?

MEEKER. *(A little irritably. From off R.)* Who is it? *(After a pause, Mr. Meeker, the bailiff, enters. There is no collar on his shirt, his hair is tousled, and there is still a bit of shaving soap on his face, which he is wiping off with a towel as he enters.)* Why, hello, Rachel. 'Scuse the way I look. *(He wipes the soap out of his ear. Then he notices her suitcase.)* Not goin' away are you? Excitement's just startin'.

RACHEL. *(Earnestly.)* Mr. Meeker, don't let my father know I came here.

MEEKER. *(Shrugs.)* The Reverend don't tell me his business. Don't know why I should tell him mine.

RACHEL. I want to see Bert Cates. Is he all right?

MEEKER. Don't know why he shouldn't be. I always figured the safest place in the world is in jail.

RACHEL. Can I go down and see him?

MEEKER. Ain't a very proper place for a minister's daughter.

RACHEL. I only want to see him for a minute.

MEEKER. Sit down, Rachel. I'll bring him up. You can talk to him right here in the courtroom. *(Rachel sits, suitcase on lap. Meeker starts out, then pauses.)* Long as I've been bailiff here, we've never had nothin' but drunks, vagrants, couple of chicken thieves. *(A little dreamily.)* Our best catch was that fella from Minnesota that chopped up his wife; we had to extradite him. *(Shakes his head.)* Seems kinda queer havin' a school-teacher in our jail. *(Shrugs.)* Might improve the writin' on the walls. *(Meeker goes out. Nervously, Rachel rises, puts suitcase down, looks around at the cold, official furnishings of the courtroom. Bert Cates enters followed by Meeker. Cates is a pale, thin young man of twenty-four. He is quiet, shy, well-mannered. Rachel and Cates face each other expressionlessly, without speaking. Meeker pauses in the doorway.)* I'll leave you two alone to talk. Don't run off, Bert. *(Meeker goes out. Rachel and Cates look at each other. There is tension between them, as if they want to rush into each other's arms.)*

RACHEL. Hello, Bert.

CATES. Rache, I told you not to come here.

RACHEL. I couldn't help it. Nobody saw me. Mr. Meeker won't tell. *(Troubled.)* I keep thinking of you, locked up here —

CATES. *(Trying to cheer her up.)* You know something funny? The food's better than the boarding house. And you'd better not tell anyone how cool it is down there, or we'll have a crime wave every summer.

RACHEL. *(Indicating suitcase.)* I stopped by your place and picked up some of your things. A clean shirt, your best tie, some handkerchiefs.

CATES. Thanks.

RACHEL. *(Rushing to him.)* Bert, why don't you tell 'em it was

11

all a joke? Tell 'em you didn't mean to break the law, and you won't do it again!

CATES. *(Breaking away from her.)* I suppose everybody's all steamed up about Brady coming.

RACHEL. He's coming in on a special train out of Chattanooga. Pa's going to the station to meet him. Everybody is!

CATES. Strike up the band.

RACHEL. *(Crossing to him.)* Bert, it's still not too late. Why can't you just admit you were wrong? If the biggest man in the country — next to the President, maybe — if Matthew Harrison Brady comes here to tell the whole world how wrong you are —

CATES. *(Turning to her.)* You still think I did wrong?

RACHEL. Why did you do it?

CATES. You know why I did it. I had the book in my hand, Hunter's *Civic Biology.* I opened it up, and read my sophomore science class Chapter 17, Darwin's *Origin of Species. (Rachel starts to protest.)* All it says is that man wasn't just stuck here like a geranium in a flower pot; that living comes from a *long* miracle, it didn't just happen in seven days.

RACHEL. There's a law against it.

CATES. I know that.

RACHEL. Everybody says what you did is bad.

CATES. It isn't as simple as that. Good or bad, black or white, night or day. Do you know, at the top of the world the twilight is six months long?

RACHEL. But we don't live at the top of the world. We live in Hillsboro, and when the sun goes down, it's dark. And why do you try to make it different? *(He turns away. Rachel gets the shirt, tie, and handkerchiefs from the suitcase.)* Here.

CATES. Thanks, Rache.

RACHEL. Why can't you be on the right side of things?

CATES. Your father's side. *(Rachel starts to close suitcase preparing to leave. Cates stops her.)* Rache — love me! *(They embrace. Meeker enters with a long-handled broom.)*

MEEKER. *(Clears his throat.)* I gotta sweep. *(Rachel breaks away and hurries off.)*

CATES. *(Calling, wanting to say "I love you.")* Thanks for the shirt! *(Meeker, who has been sweeping impassively, stops and leans on the broom.)*

MEEKER. Imagine. Matthew Harrison Brady comin' here. I voted for him for President. Twice. In nineteen-hundred, and again in oh-eight. Wasn't old enough to vote for him the first time he ran. But my Pa did. *(Turns proudly to Cates.)* I *seen* him once. At a Chautauqua meeting in Chattanooga. *(Impressed, remembering, booming it.)* The tent-poles shook! *(Cates moves nervously.)* Who's gonna be your lawyer, son?

CATES. I don't know yet. I wrote to that newspaper in Baltimore. They're sending somebody.

MEEKER. *(Resumes sweeping.)* He better be loud.

CATES. *(Picking up the shirt.)* You want me to go back down?

MEEKER. No need. You can stay up here if you want.

CATES. *(Going toward the jail.)* I'm supposed to be in jail; I'd better be in jail! *(Meeker shrugs and follows Cates off. The action is continuous as the lights fade in the courtroom area, coming up at the same time on the town: morning of a hot July day. Mr. Goodfellow, the haberdasher, enters, unlocking his store. Mrs. Krebs saunters across the square, fanning herself.)*

MR. GOODFELLOW. Warm enough for you, Mrs. Krebs?

MRS. KREBS. The good Lord gave us the heat, and the good Lord gave us the glands to sweat with.

MR. GOODFELLOW. I bet the Devil ain't so obliging.

MRS. KREBS. I don't intend to find out. *(The Reverend Jeremiah Brown strides on. He looks around, scowling.)*

MR. GOODFELLOW. Good morning, Reverend.

BROWN. 'Morning.

MRS. KREBS. 'Morning, Reverend.

BROWN. Mrs. Krebs. *(Shouting off.)* Where's the banner? Why haven't you raised the banner?

SILLERS. *(Enters followed by Phil, another workman. They carry a canvas banner between them.)* Paint didn't dry till just now.

BROWN. See that you have it up before Mr. Brady arrives. *(Cooper enters, greets Mrs. Krebs.)*

SILLERS. Fast as we can do it, Reverend.

BROWN. We must show him at once what kind of a community this is.

SILLERS. Yes, Reverend. Come on, Phil. Hep. *(They proceed to hang banner, which says: "Read your Bible.")*

KREBS. Big day, Reverend.

BROWN. Indeed it is. Picnic lunch ready, Mrs. Krebs?

MRS. KREBS. Fit'n for a king.

BOLLINGER. *(Running on, carrying his cornet.)* Station master says old Ninety-four's on time out of Chattanooga. Brady's on board all right. *(Krebs, Dunlap and Bannister enter, greet the Reverend.)*

COOPER. The minute Brady gets here, people are gonna pour in. Town's gonna fill up like a rain barrel in a flood.

GOODFELLOW. That means business. *(Mrs. Loomis and her daughter Melinda enter. Mrs. Loomis carries a lemonade pitcher and sign, Melinda carries a lemonade stand. They proceed to set it up.)*

BANNISTER. Where they gonna stay? Where we gonna sleep all them people?

KREBS. They got money, we'll sleep 'em.

DUNLAP. Looks like the biggest day for this town since we put up Coxey's Army.

HOWARD. *(Bolting on.)* Hey! Ted Finney's got out his big bass drum. And you ought to see what they done to the depot. Ribbons all over the rain spouts.

MELINDA. Lemonade! Lemonade! *(Mrs. Blair enters, looking for Howard. She stops at lemonade stand and talks with Mrs. Loomis.)*

SILLERS. *(Who, with Phil, has finally raised the banner over the courthouse door, calls out to the Reverend.)* It's all ready, Reverend! *(All focus on the banner. Applause, cheers. Bollinger blows a ragged fanfare.)*

HOT DOG MAN. *(Selling hot dogs from a wagon or from box he carries.)* Hot dogs. Get your red hots. Hot dogs. *(Doc Kimble comes out of his drug store.)*

MRS. McLAIN. *(Carrying a shopping bag full of frond fans, enters.)* Get your fans, compliments of Maley's Funeral Home, 35 cents.

MELINDA. Lemonade! Lemonade!

MRS. BLAIR. *(Who has spotted her son.)* Howard! Howard!

HOWARD. *(Racing to her.)* Hey, Ma. This is just like the county fair.

MRS. BLAIR. Now you settle down and stop runnin' around and pay some attention when Mr. Brady gets here. Spit down your hair. *(Howard spits in her hand, and she pastes down a cowlick.)* Hold still! *(Howard flashes off through the crowd. Elijah, a "holy man" from the hills, comes on with a wooden vegetable crate full of books. He is bearded, wild-haired, dressed in a tattered burlap smock. His feet are bare. He sets up shop between the hot dogs and the lemonade, with a placard reading: "Where will you spend eternity?")*

ELIJAH. *(In a shrill, screeching voice.)* Buy a Bible! Your guide-book to eternal life! *(E.K. Hornbeck wanders on, carrying a suitcase. He is a newspaperman in his middle thirties, who sneers politely at everything, including himself. His clothes — those of a sophisticated city-dweller — contrast sharply with the attire of the townspeople. He uses his "boater" straw-hat throughout as kind of an impertinent prop. Still unnoticed by most of the townspeople, Hornbeck looks around with wonderful contempt.)*

MRS. McLAIN. *(To Hornbeck.)* Want a fan? Compliments of Maley's Funeral Home — thirty-five cents!

HORNBECK. I'd die first.

MRS. KREBS. *(Unctuously, to Hornbeck.)* You're a stranger, aren't you, mister? Want a nice clean place to stay?

HORNBECK. I had a nice clean place to stay, madame. And I left it to come here.

MRS. KREBS. *(Undaunted.)* You're gonna need a room.

HORNBECK. I have a reservation at the Mansion House.

MRS. KREBS. Oh? *(She sniffs.)* That's all right, I suppose, for them as *likes* having a privy practically in the bedroom. *(She turns away from him. He tips his straw hat to her.)*

HORNBECK. The unplumbed and plumbing-less depths. Ahhh, Hillsboro, Heavenly Hillsboro, the buckle on the Bible belt. *(The Hot Dog Man and Elijah converge on Hornbeck from opposite sides.)*

HOT DOG MAN. Hot dog?

ELIJAH. Buy a Bible?

HORNBECK. *(Up ends his suitcase and sits on it.)* Now that poses a pretty problem. Which is hungrier — my stomach or my soul? *(Buys hot dog.)* My stomach. *(Hot Dog Man accepts money from Hornbeck and moves off.)*

ELIJAH. *(Miffed)* What are you? An evolutionist? An infidel? A sinner?

HORNBECK. *(Munching on hot dog.)* The worst kind. I write for a newspaper. *(Hornbeck offers his hand.)* I'm E.K. Hornbeck, Baltimore *Herald*. I don't believe I caught your name.

ELIJAH. *(Impressively, not taking his hand.)* They call me ... Elijah.

HORNBECK. *(Pleased.)* Elijah. Yes. Why, I had no idea you were still around. I've read some of your stuff.

ELIJAH. *(Haughtily.)* I neither read nor write.

HORNBECK. Oh. Excuse me. I must be thinking of another Elijah. *(An organ grinder enters, with a live monkey on a string. Hornbeck spies the monkey gleefully; he greets the monk with arms outstretched.)* Grandpa! *(Crosses to the monkey, bends down and shakes the monkey's hand.)* Welcome to Hillsboro, sir! Have you come to testify for the defense? Or for the prosecution? *(The monkey, oddly enough, doesn't answer.)* No comment? That's fairly safe. But I warn you, sir. You can't compete with all these monkeyshines. *(Melinda hands the monkey a penny.)*

MELINDA. Look! He took my penny!

HORNBECK. How could you ask for better proof than that? *There's* the father of the human race!

TIMMY. *(Running on breathlessly.)* Train's coming! I seen the smoke 'way up the track!

BROWN. All the members of the Bible League, get ready. Let us show Mr. Brady the spirit with which we welcome him to Hillsboro! *(The crowd lets out a mighty cheer. Mrs. Blair blows a note on her pitch-pipe and sings the first line of "Marching to Zion.")*

MRS. BLAIR. *(Singing.)*

"We're marching to Zion"

ALL. *(Taking up the song.)*

— Beautiful, beautiful Zion.

(Mrs. Blair waves the crowd to follow her. The crowd marches off singing.)

We're marching upwards to Zion,

The beautiful city of God.

(Hornbeck turns to watch the last of the crowd disappear. Even the organ grinder leaves his monkey tied to the hurdy-gurdy and joins the departing crowd.)

HORNBECK. Amen! *(To the monkey.)* Shield your eyes, monk,

you are about to meet the mightiest of your descendants. A man who wears a cathedral for a cloak and a church spire for a hat. Whose tread has the thunder of the legions of the lion hearted.

CROWD. *(Offstage, singing.)* Let those refuse to sing
  Who never knew our God
  But children of the Heavenly King
  But children of the Heavenly King
  Shall shout their joys abroad.
  We're marching to Zion *(etc.)*

(Mr. Goodfellow, the storekeeper, emerges from his establishment and looks in his own store window. Hornbeck turns to him.)

HORNBECK. Hey, you're missing the show.

GOODFELLOW. Somebody's got to mind the store.

HORNBECK. May I ask your opinion, sir, on the subject of evolution?

GOODFELLOW. Don't have any opinions. They're bad for business. *(Offstage, a cheer. Then the thumping drum into "Gimme That Old-Time Religion" sung by the unseen townspeople.)*

HORNBECK. *(To the monkey.)* Sound the trumpet, beat the drum. Everybody's come to town to see your competition, monk. Alive and breathing in the county cooler: a high-school teacher — wild, untamed! *(The crowd surges back, augmented, in a jubilant parade. Many are carrying banners, reading:*

ARE YOU A MAN OR A MONKEY?
AMEND THE CONSTITUTION — PROHIBIT DARWIN
SAVE OUR SCHOOLS FROM SIN
MY ANCESTORS AIN'T APES!
WELCOME, MATTHEW HARRISON BRADY
DOWN WITH DARWIN
BE A SWEET ANGEL
DON'T MONKEY WITH OUR SCHOOLS!
DARWIN IS WRONG!
DOWN WITH EVOLUTION
DO YOU WANT WINGS OR HORNS?

(Hornbeck goes to the background to watch the show. Matthew Harrison Brady comes on, a benign giant of a man, wearing a pith helmet. He basks in the cheers and the excitement, like a patriarch surrounded by his children. He is balding, paunchy, an indeterminate

sixty-five. He is followed by Mrs. Brady, the Mayor, Reverend Brown,
Tom Davenport, the circuit district attorney, some newspapermen,
and an army of the curious.)
ALL. *(Singing.)*

> Gimme that old-time religion,
> Gimme that old-time religion,
> Gimme that old-time religion,
> It's good enough for me!
>
> It was good enough for father,
> It was good enough for father,
> It was good enough for father,
> And it's good enough for me!
>
> It was good for the Hebrew children,
> It was good for the Hebrew children,
> It was good for the Hebrew children,
> And it's good enough for me!
>
> Gimme that old time religion,
> Gimme that old time religion,
> Gimme that old time religion,
> It's good enough for me!

REVEREND. *(Speaks.)* It is good enough for Brady!
ALL. *(Singing)*

> It is good enough for Brady,
> It is good enough for Brady,
> And it's good enough for me!

(Cheers and applause. Brady seems to carry with him a built-in spot-
light. So Mrs. Brady — pretty, fashionably dressed, a proper "Second
Lady" to the nation's "Second Man" — seems always to be in his shad-
ow. This does not annoy her. Sarah Brady is content that all her
thoughts and emotions should gain the name of action through her
husband. Brady removes his hat and raises his hand. Obediently, the
crowd falls to a hushed anticipatory silence.)
BRADY. Friends — and I can see most of you are my friends,
from the way you have decked out your beautiful city of Hillsboro.
(There is a pleased reaction, and a spattering of applause. When Brady

18

speaks, there can be no doubt of his personal magnetism. Even Hornbeck, who slouches contemptuously, is impressed with the speaker's power, for here is a man to be reckoned with.) Mrs. Brady and I are delighted to be among you! *(Brady takes his wife's hand and draws her to his side, then mops his brow.)* I could only wish one thing: that you had not given us *quite* so warm a welcome! *(Brady removes his alpaca coat. Goodfellow takes it. The crowd laughs. Brady beams. Mrs. McLain hands him a frond fan. Brady takes it.)* Bless you. *(He fans himself vigorously.)* My friends of Hillsboro, you know why I have come here. Not merely to prosecute a lawbreaker, an arrogant youth who has spoken out against the Revealed Word, but to defend that which is most precious in the hearts of all of us: the Living Truth of the Scriptures! *(Applause and cheering.)*

PHOTOGRAPHER. *(Topping the cheer.)* Mr. Brady. A picture, Mr. Brady?

BRADY. I shall be happy to oblige! *(To his wife.)* Sarah ...

MRS. BRADY. *(Moving out of camera range.)* No, Matt. Just you and the dignitaries.

BRADY. You are the Mayor, are you not, sir?

MAYOR. *(Stepping forward, awkwardly.)* I am, sir.

BRADY. *(Extending his hand.)* My name is Matthew Harrison Brady.

MAYOR. Oh, I know. Everybody knows that. I had a little speech of welcome ready, but somehow it didn't seem necessary.

BRADY. I shall be honored to hear your greeting, sir. *(The Mayor clears his throat and takes his speech from his pocket.)*

MAYOR. *(Sincerely.)* Mr. Matthew Harrison Brady, this municipality is proud to have within its city limits the warrior who has always fought for us ordinary people. The lady folks of this town wouldn't have the vote if it wasn't for you, fightin' to give 'em all that suffrage. Mr. President Wilson wouldn't never have got to the White House and won the war if it wasn't for you supportin' him. And, in conclusion, the Governor of our state ... *(His hand is raised.)*

PHOTOGRAPHER. Hold it! *(The camera clicks.)* Thank you. *(Mrs .Brady is disturbed by the informality of the pose.)*

MRS. BRADY. Matt — you didn't have your coat on.

BRADY. *(To the photographer.)* Perhaps we should have a more

19

formal pose. *(As Mrs. Brady helps him on with his coat.)* Who is the spiritual leader of the community?

MAYOR.   That would be the Reverend Jeremiah Brown. *(Reverend Brown steps forward.)*

BROWN.   Your servant, and the Lord's. *(Brady and Brown shake hands.)*

BRADY.   The Reverend at my left, the Mayor at my right. *(Stiffly, they face the camera.)* We must look grave, gentlemen, but not too serious. Hopeful, I think is the word. We must look hopeful. *(Brady assumes the familiar oratorical pose. The camera clicks. Unnoticed, Howard has stuck his head, mouth agape, into the picture. The Mayor refers to the last page of his undelivered speech.)*

MAYOR.   In conclusion, the Governor of our state has vested in me the authority to confer upon you a commission as Honorary Colonel in the State Militia. *(Applause.)*

BRADY.   *(Savoring it.)* "Colonel Brady." I like the sound of that!

BROWN.   We thought you might be hungry, Colonel Brady, after your train ride.

MAYOR.   So the members of our Ladies' Aid have prepared a buffet lunch.

BRADY.   Splendid, splendid — I could do with a little snack. *(Some of the townspeople, at Brown's direction, carry on a long picnic table, loaded with foodstuffs, potato salad, fried turkey, pickled fruits, cold meats and all the picnic paraphernalia. Rachel comes on following the table, carrying a pitcher of lemonade which she places on the table.)*

BANNISTER.   *(An eager beaver.)* You know, Mr. Brady — *Colonel* Brady — all of us here voted for you three times.

BRADY.   I trust it was in three separate elections! *(There is laughter. Tom Davenport, a crisp, businesslike young man, offers his hand to Brady.)*

DAVENPORT.   Sir, I'm Tom Davenport.

BRADY.   *(Beaming.)* Of course. Circuit district attorney. *(Putting his arm around Davenport's shoulder.)* We'll be a team, won't we, young man! Quite a team! *(The picnic table is in place. The sight of the food being uncovered is a magnetic attraction to Brady. He beams, and moistens his lips.)* Ahhhh, what a handsome repast! *(Some of the women grin sheepishly at the flattery. Brady is a great eater. And he piles mountains of food on his plate.)* What a challenge it is, to fit on the old armor again! To test the steel of our Truth against the blasphemies of Science! To stand —

MRS. BRADY. Matthew, it's a warm day. Remember, the doctor told you not to overeat.

BRADY. Don't worry, Mother. Just a bite or two. *(He hoists a huge drumstick on his plate, then assails a mountain of potato salad.)* Who among you knows the defendants? — Cates, is that his name?

DAVENPORT. Well we *all* know him, sir.

MAYOR. Just about everybody in Hillsboro knows everybody else.

BRADY. Can someone tell me — is this fellow Cates a criminal by nature?

RACHEL. *(Almost involuntarily.)* Bert isn't a criminal. He's good, really. He's just — *(Rachel seems to shrink from the attention that centers on her. She takes an empty bowl and starts off with it.)*

BRADY. Wait, my child. Is Mr. Cates your friend?

RACHEL. *(Looking down, trying to get away.)* I can't tell you anything about him —

BROWN. *(Fiercely.)* Rachel! *(To Brady.)* My daughter will be pleased to answer any questions about Bertram Cates.

BRADY. Your daughter, Reverend? You must be proud, indeed. *(Brown nods. Brady takes a mouthful of potato salad, turns to Rachel.)* Now. How did you come to be acquainted with Mr. Cates?

RACHEL. *(Suffering.)* At school. I'm a schoolteacher, too.

BRADY. I'm sure you teach according to the precepts of the Lord.

RACHEL. I try. My pupils are only second-graders.

BRADY. Has Mr. Cates ever tried to pollute your mind with his heathen dogma?

RACHEL. Bert isn't a heathen!

BRADY. *(Sympathetically.)* I understand your loyalty, my child. This man, the man in your jailhouse, is a fellow schoolteacher. Likeable, no doubt. And you are loath to speak out against him before all these people. *(Brady takes her arm, still carrying his plate. He moves her easily away from the others. As they move.)* Think of me as a friend, Rachel. And tell me what troubles you. *(Brady moves her upstage and their conversation continues, inaudible to us. Brady continues to eat. Rachel speaks to him earnestly. The townspeople stand around the picnic table, munching the buffet lunch.)*

BANNISTER. Who's gonna be the defense attorney?

DAVENPORT. We don't know yet. It hasn't been announced.

MAYOR. *(Turning to Mrs. Brady.)* Well, whoever he is, he won't have much chance against your husband, will he, Mrs. Brady? *(Crowd laughs.)*

HORNBECK. I disagree. *(The crowd quiets.)*

MAYOR. Who are you?

HORNBECK. Hornbeck. E.K. Hornbeck of the Baltimore *Herald.*

BROWN. *(Can't quite place the name but it has unpleasant connotations.)* Hornbeck? Hornbeck?

HORNBECK. I am a newspaper man, bearing news. When this sovereign state determined to indict the sovereign mind of a less than sovereign schoolteacher, my editor decided there was more than a headline here. The Baltimore *Herald*, therefore, is happy to announce that it is sending *two* representatives to "Heavenly Hillsboro" — the most brilliant journalist in America today — *(Tipping his hat.)* myself. *(Crowd snickers.)* And the most agile legal mind of the 20th century — Henry Drummond. *(This name is like a whipcrack. Hornbeck moves easily to the picnic tables.)*

MRS. BRADY. *(Stunned.)* Drummond —

BROWN. Henry Drummond, the agnostic?

BANNISTER. I heard about him. He got them two Chicago child-murderers off, just the other day.

BROWN. A vicious, godless man. *(Blithely, Hornbeck, having inspected the food, chooses a drumstick. He waves it jauntily toward the astonished party.)*

HORNBECK. A Merry Christmas and a jolly Fourth of July! *(Munching the drumstick, he gets his suitcase and exits. Brady and Rachel, having left the scene, have missed this significant disclosure. There is a stunned pause.)*

DAVENPORT. *(Genuinely impressed.)* Henry Drummond for the defense. Well!

BROWN. Henry Drummond is an agent of darkness. We won't allow him in this town.

DAVENPORT. I don't know by what law you can keep him out.

MAYOR. I could look it up in the town ordinances.

BROWN. I saw Drummond once. In a courtroom in Ohio. A man was on trial for a most brutal crime. Although he knew and admitted the man was guilty, Drummond was perverting the evidence to turn the guilt away from the accused and on to you and me — and all of society.

MRS. BRADY. Henry Drummond. Oh, dear me.

BROWN. I can still see him. A slouching hulk of a man, whose head juts out like an animal's. *(He imitates Drummond's slouch. Melinda watches, frightened.)* You look into his face, and you wonder why God made such a man. And then you know that God didn't make him, that he is a creature of the Devil, perhaps even the Devil himself! *(Little Melinda utters a frightened cry, and buries her head in the folds of her mother's skirt. Brady re-enters with Rachel, who has a confused and guilty look. Brady's plate has been scraped clean; only the fossil of the turkey leg remains. He looks at the ring of faces, which have been disturbed by Brown's description of the heretic Drummond. Mrs. Brady comes toward him.)*

MRS. BRADY. Matt — they're bringing Henry Drummond for the defense.

BRADY. *(Pale.)* Drummond? *(The townspeople are impressed by the impact of this name on Brady.)* Henry Drummond!

BROWN. We won't allow him in the town!

MAYOR. *(Lamely.)* I think — maybe the Board of Health — *(He trails off.)*

BRADY. *(Crossing thoughtfully.)* No. *(He turns.)* I believe we should *welcome* Henry Drummond.

MAYOR. *(Astonished.)* Welcome him!

BRADY. If the enemy sends its Goliath into battle, it magnifies our cause. Henry Drummond has stalked the courtrooms of this land for forty years. When he fights, headlines follow. *(With growing fervor.)* The whole world will be watching our victory over Drummond. *(Dramatically.)* If St. George had slain a drago*nfly*, who would remember him? *(Cheers and pleased reactions from the crowd.)*

MRS. BLAIR. Would you care to finish off the pickled apricots, Mr. Brady? *(Brady takes them.)*

BRADY. It would be a pity to see them go to waste.

MRS. BRADY. Matt, do you think — ?

BRADY. Have to build up my strength, Mother, for the battle

ahead. *(Munching thoughtfully.)* Now what will Drummond do? He'll try to make us forget the lawbreaker and put the law on trail. *(He turns to Rachel.)* But we'll have the *answer* for Mr. Drummond. Right here, in some of the things this sweet young lady has told me.

RACHEL. But Mr. Brady — *(Brady turns to Brown.)*

BRADY. A fine girl, Reverend. Fine girl! *(Rachel seems tormented, but helpless.)*

BROWN. Rachel has always been taught to do the righteous thing. *(Rachel moves off.)*

BRADY. I'm sure she has. *(Melinda hands him a glass of lemonade.)* Thank you. A toast, then! A toast to tomorrow! To the beginning of the trial and the success of our cause. A toast, in good American lemonade! *(Brady downs his drink. Cheers and applause.)*

MRS. BRADY. Mr. Mayor, it's time for Mr. Brady's nap. He always likes to nap after a meal.

MAYOR. We have a suite ready for you at the Mansion House. I think you'll find your bags already there.

BRADY. Very thoughtful, considerate of you.

MAYOR. If you'll come with me — it's only across the square. *(They start off. Brady turns.)*

BRADY. I want to thank all the members of the Ladies' Aid for preparing this nice little picnic repast.

MRS. KREBS. *(Beaming.)* Our pleasure, sir.

BRADY. And if I seemed to pick at my food, I don't want you to think I didn't enjoy it. *(Apologetically.)* But you see, we had a box lunch on the train. *(There is a good-humored reaction to this, and the Bradys move off accompanied by the throng of admirers, singing "It is good enough for Brady." Simultaneously the lights fade on the courthouse lawn and come up on the dimly-lit courtroom area. Hornbeck saunters on, chewing at an apple. He glances about the courtroom as if he were searching for something. When Rachel hurries on, Hornbeck drops back into a shadow and she does not see him.)*

RACHEL. *(Distressed)* Mr. Meeker. Mr. Meeker? *(She calls down toward the jail.)* Bert, can you hear me? Bert, you've got to tell me what to do. I don't know what to do — *(Hornbeck takes a bite out of his apple. Rachel turns sharply at the sound, surprised to find someone else in the courtroom.)*

24

HORNBECK. *(Quietly.)* I give advice, at remarkably low hourly rates. Ten percent off to unmarried young ladies. And special discounts to the clergy and their daughters.

RACHEL. What are you doing here?

HORNBECK. I'm inspecting the battlefield — the night before the battle. Before it's cluttered with the debris of journalistic camp-followers. *(Hiking himself up on a window ledge.)* I'm scouting myself an observation post to watch the fray. *(Rachel starts to go off.)* Wait. Why do you want to see Bert Cates? What's he to you, or you to him? Can it be that both beauty and biology are on our side? *(Again she starts to leave. But Hornbeck jumps down from his ledge and crosses toward her.)* There's a newspaper here I'd like to have you see. It just arrived from that wicked modern Sodom and Gomorrah: Baltimore! *(Rachel looks at him quizzically as he fishes a tear sheet out of his picket.)* Not the entire edition, of course. No Happy Hooligan, Barney Google, Abe Kabibble. Merely the part worth reading: E.K. Hornbeck's brilliant little symphony of words. *(He offers her the sheet, but she doesn't take it.)* You should read it. *(Almost reluctantly, she starts to read.)* My typewriter's been singing a sweet, sad song about the Hillsboro heretic, B. Cates: boy-Socrates, latter-day Dreyfus, Romeo with a biology book. *(He looks over her shoulder, admiring his own writing. He takes another bite out of the apple.)* I may be rancid butter, but I'm on your side of the bread.

RACHEL. *(Looking up, surprised.)* This sounds as if you're a friend of Bert's.

HORNBECK. As much as a critic can be a friend to anyone. *(He takes another bite out of his apple, then offers it to her.)* Have a bite? *(Rachel, busily reading, shakes her head.)* Don't worry. I'm not the serpent, Little Eva. This isn't from the Tree of Knowledge. You won't find one in the orchards of Heavenly Hillsboro. Birches, beeches, butternuts. A few ignorance bushes. No Tree of Knowledge. *(Rachel has finished reading the copy; and she looks up at Hornbeck with a new respect.)*

RACHEL. Will this be published here, in the local paper?

HORNBECK. In the "Weekly Bugle"? Or whatever it is they call the leaden stuff they blow through the local linotypes? I doubt it.

RACHEL. It would help Bert if the people here could read this. It would help them understand...! *(She appraises Hornbeck, puzzled.)* I never would have expected you to write an article like this. You seem so —

HORNBECK. *(Swallows before he can get the word out.)* Cynical? That's my fascination. I do hateful things, for which people love me, and lovable things for which they hate me. I am the friend of enemies, the enemy of friends. I am admired for my detestability. I am both Poles and the Equator, with no Temperate Zones in between.

RACHEL. *(Looking up from the copy.)* You make it sound as if Bert is a hero. I'd like to think that, but I can't. A schoolteacher is a public servant: I think he should do what the law and the school board want him to. If the superintendent comes to me and says, "Miss Brown, you're to teach from Whitley's Second Reader," I don't feel I have to give him an argument.

HORNBECK. *(Crossing to her.)* Ever give your pupils a snap-quiz on existence?

RACHEL. *(Turning to him.)* What?

HORNBECK. Where we are, where we came from, where we're going?

RACHEL. *(Turning away.)* All the answers to those questions are in the Bible.

HORNBECK. *(With genuine incredulity.)* All?! You feed the youth of Hillsboro from the little truck-garden of your mind?

RACHEL. I think there must be something wrong in what Bert believes, if a great man like Mr. Brady comes here to speak out against him.

HORNBECK. Matthew Harrison Brady came here to find himself a stump to shout from. That's all.

RACHEL. You couldn't understand. Mr. Brady is the champion of ordinary people, like us.

HORNBECK. Wake up, Sleeping Beauty. The ordinary people played a dirty trick on Colonel Brady. They ceased to exist. *(Rachel looks puzzled.)* Time was when Colonel Brady was the hero of the hinterland. Water-boy for the great unwashed. But they've got *inside-plumbing* in their heads these days. There's a highway through the backwoods now; and the trees of the forest have reluctantly made room for their leafless cousins, the telephone poles.

26

Henry's Lizzie rattles into town, and leaves behind the Yesterday-Messiah — standing in the road alone, in a cloud of flivver dust. *(Emphatically, he brandishes the apple.)* The boob has been *de-boobed.* Colonel Brady's virginal small-towner has been *had* — *(She starts to leave.)* By Marconi. And Montgomery Ward. *(Offering the apple again.)* Sure you don't want a bite? Awful good. *(Hornbeck strolls out of the courtroom and up onto the town square. The action is continuous, without pause, as the lights dissolve from one area to the other. Rachel stares after Hornbeck, not knowing quite what to make of this strange man, then she moves off. The store-fronts in the town glow with sunset light. Goodfellow pulls the shade in his store window and locks the door. Mrs. McLain crosses the square, fanning herself wearily.)*
STOREKEEPER. Gonna be a hot night, Mrs. McLain.
MRS. McLAIN. I thought we'd get some relief when the sun went down. *(Hornbeck tosses away his apple core, then leans back and watches as the shopkeeper and Mrs. McLain go off. The organ-grinder comes on, idly, with his monkey. Melinda enters, attracted by the melody which tinkles in the twilight. She gives the monkey a penny. The organ-grinder thanks her, and moves off. Melinda is alone, back to the audience, in center stage. Hornbeck, silent and motionless, watches from the side. The faces of the buildings are now red with the dying moment of sunset. A long, ominous shadow appears across the buildings, cast from a figure approaching offstage. Melinda awed, watches the shadow grow. Henry Drummond enters, carrying a valise. He is hunched over, head jutting forward, exactly as Brown described him. The red of the sun behind him hits his slouching back, and his face is in shadow. Melinda turns and looks at Drummond, full in the face.)*
MELINDA. *(Terrified.)* It's the Devil! *(Screaming with fear, Melinda runs off. Hornbeck crosses slowly toward Drummond, and offers his hand.)*
HORNBECK. Hello, Devil. Welcome to Hell. *(The lights fade.)*

Scene 2

The Courtroom. A few days later.

In the momentary dark, the courtroom fills up. Suddenly the lights bump on to full: a freeze-frame, the sharp afternoon sun flooding through the windows, a moment caught in amber, then springing to life.

The townspeople are packed into the sweltering courtroom. The shapes of the buildings are dimly visible in the background, as if Hillsboro itself were on trial. Court is in session, fans are pumping. The humorless judge sits at his bench; he has a nervous habit of flashing an automatic smile after every ruling. Cates sits beside Drummond at a counsel table. Brady sits grandly at another table, fanning himself with benign self-assurance. Hornbeck is seated on his window ledge. Rachel, tense, is among the spectators. In the jury box, ten of the twelve jurors are already seated. Bannister is on the witness stand. Davenport is examining him.

DAVENPORT. Do you attend church regularly, Mr. Bannister?

BANNISTER. Only on Sundays.

DAVENPORT. That's good enough for the prosecution. Your Honor, we will accept this man as a member of the jury. *(Bannister starts toward the jury box.)*

JUDGE. One moment, Mr. Bannister. You're not excused.

BANNISTER. *(A little petulant.)* I wanted that there front seat in the jury box.

DRUMMOND. *(Rising.)* Well, hold your horses, Bannister. You may get it yet!

JUDGE. Mr. Drummond, you may examine the venireman.

DRUMMOND. *(Crossing.)* Thank you, your honor. Mr. Bannister, how come you're so anxious to get that front seat over there?

BANNISTER. Everybody says this is going to be quite a show. *(Spectators laugh.)*

DRUMMOND. I hear the same thing. Ever read anything in a book about evolution?

BANNISTER. Nope.

DRUMMOND. Or about a fellow named Darwin?

BANNISTER. Can't say I have.

DRUMMOND. I'll bet you read your Bible.

BANNISTER. Nope.

DRUMMOND. How come...?

BANNISTER. I can't read. *(Spectators laugh.)*

DRUMMOND. Well, you are fortunate. *(There are a few titters through the courtroom. Drummond crosses to his table.)* He'll do. *(Bannister turns toward the Judge, poised.)*

JUDGE. Take your seat, Mr. Bannister. *(Bannister races to the jury box as if shot from a gun, and sits in the front row seat, beaming.)* Mr. Meeker, will you call a venireman to fill the twelfth and last seat on the jury? *(Meeker crosses to the spectators.)*

BRADY. *(Rising.)* Your Honor, before we continue, will the court entertain a motion on a matter of procedure?

JUDGE. Will the learned prosecutor state the motion?

MEEKER. Jesse H. Dunlap. You're next, Jesse.

BRADY. It has been called to my attention that the temperature is now 97 degrees Fahrenheit. *(He mops his forehead with a large handkerchief. Dunlap goes to the witness stand, sits. Meeker returns to his chair.)* And it may get hotter! *(There is laughter. Brady basks in the warmth of his popularity.)* I do not feel that the dignity of the court will suffer if we remove a few superfluous outer garments. *(Brady indicates his alpaca coat.)*

JUDGE. Does the defense object to Colonel Brady's motion?

DRUMMOND. *(Askance.)* I don't know if the dignity of the court can be upheld with these galluses I've got on.

JUDGE. Well — we'll take that chance, Mr. Drummond. Those who wish to remove their coats may do so. *(With relief, all except the Judge take off their coats and loosen their collar buttons. Drummond removes his coat, drapes it over back of his chair — as does Brady. Drummond wears wide, lavender suspenders. The specta-*

tors react.)

BRADY. *(With affable sarcasm.)* Is the counsel for defense showing us the latest fashion in the great metropolitan city of Chicago?

DRUMMOND. *(Pleased.)* I'm glad you asked me that. I brought these along special. *(He cocks his thumbs in the suspenders.)* It just so happens I bought these galluses at Peabody's General Store in *your* home town, Mr. Brady. Weeping Water, Nebraska. *(Drummond snaps the suspenders jauntily. There is amused reaction at this. Brady is nettled: This is his show, and he wants all the laughs. The Judge pounds for order. Drummond and Brady sit.)*

JUDGE. Let us proceed with the selection of the final juror. *(Dunlap is a rugged, righteous-looking man.)*

MEEKER. State your name and occupation.

DUNLAP. Jesse H. Dunlap. Farmer and cabinet-maker.

DAVENPORT. Do you believe in the Bible, Mr. Dunlap?

DUNLAP. *(Vigorously, almost shouting.)* I believe in the Holy Word of God. And I believe in Matthew Harrison Brady! *(There is strong applause, and a few scattered "Amens" from spectators.)*

DAVENPORT. *(Crossing to his table.)* This man is acceptable to the prosecution. *(He sits.)*

JUDGE. Very well. Mr. Drummond?

DRUMMOND. *(Quietly, without rising.)* No questions, not acceptable.

BRADY. *(Annoyed, rising.)* Does Mr. Drummond refuse this man a place on the jury simply because he believes in the Bible?

DRUMMOND. If you can find an Evolutionist in this town, you can refuse him!

BRADY. *(Turning to Judge, angrily.)* Your Honor. I object to the Defense Attorney rejecting a worthy citizen without so much as asking him a question! *(Crowd mutters angrily.)*

DRUMMOND. *(Agreeably.)* All right. I'll ask him a question. *(Saunters over to Dunlap with deliberate slowness, stops.)* How are you?

DUNLAP. *(A little surprised.)* Kinda hot.

DRUMMOND. So am I. Excused. *(Dunlap looks at the Judge, confused, as Drummond crosses back to his table and sits.)*

JUDGE. You are excused from jury duty, Mr. Dunlap. You may step down. *(Meeker waves Dunlap back and he joins the spectators, a little miffed.)*

BRADY. *(Rising piously.)* I object to the note of levity which the counsel for the defense is introducing into these proceedings.

JUDGE. The bench agrees with you in spirit, Colonel Brady.

DRUMMOND. *(Rising angrily.)* And *I* object to all this damned "Colonel" talk. I am not familiar with Mr. Brady's military record.

JUDGE. Well — he was made an Honorary Colonel in our state militia. The day he arrived in Hillsboro.

DRUMMOND. The use of this title prejudices the case of my client: it calls up a picture of the prosecution, astride a white horse, ablaze in the uniform of a militia colonel, with all the forces of right and righteousness marshalled behind him.

JUDGE. Well, what are we to do?

DRUMMOND. Break him. Make him a Private. *(Sits.)* I have no serious objection to the honorary title of "Private Brady." *(There is a buzz of reaction. The Judge gestures for the Mayor to come over for a hurried, whispered conference.)*

MAYOR. *(After some whispering.)* Well, we can't take it back — ! *(There is another whispered exchange. Then the Mayor steps gingerly toward Drummond.)* By — by authority of — well, I'm sure the Governor won't have any objection — I hereby appoint you, Mr. Drummond, a temporary Honorary Colonel in the State Militia.

DRUMMOND. *(Rises, shaking his head, with mock humility.)* Gentlemen, I don't know what to say. It is not often in a man's life that he attains the exalted rank of "Temporary Honorary Colonel."

MAYOR. *(Shaking hands.)* It will be made permanent, of course, pending the arrival of the proper papers over the Governor's signature. *(Meeker leads Sillers to the witness stand and returns to his chair.)*

DRUMMOND. *(Looking at the floor.)* I thank you. *(Mayor crosses back to his chair and sits.)*

JUDGE. Colonel Brady. *Colonel* Drummond. You will examine the venireman. *(Davenport moves to the witness.)*

MEEKER. State your name and occupation.

SILLERS. George Sillers. I work at the feed store.

DAVENPORT. Tell me, sir. Would you call yourself a religious man?

SILLERS. I guess I'm as religious as the next man. *(Brady rises.*

Davenport immediately steps back, deferring to his superior.)

BRADY. In Hillsboro, sir, that means a great deal. *(Crossing to Sillers.)* Tell me, do you have any children, Mr. Sillers?

SILLERS. Not as I know of. *(The crowd titters.)*

BRADY. If you had a son, Mr. Sillers, or a daughter, what would you think if that sweet child came home from school and told you that a Godless teacher —

DRUMMOND. *(Rising.)* Objection! We're supposed to be choosing jury members! The prosecution's denouncing the defendant before the trial has even begun!

JUDGE. Objection sustained. *(The Judge and Brady exchange meaningless smiles. Drummond sits.)*

BRADY. Mr. Sillers. Do you have any personal opinions with regard to the defendant that might prejudice you on his behalf?

SILLERS. Cates? I don't hardly know him. He did buy some peat moss from me once, and paid his bill.

BRADY. Mr. Sillers impresses me as an honest, God-fearing man. I accept him. *(He returns to his seat. Davenport, on his way back to his seat, whispers to Brady, then sits.)*

JUDGE. Thank you, Colonel Brady. *Colonel* Drummond?

DRUMMOND. *(Strolling toward the witness chair.)* Mr. Sillers, I just heard you say that you were a religious man. Tell me something. Do you work at it very hard?

SILLERS. Well, I'm pretty busy down at the feed store. My wife tends to the religion for both of us.

DRUMMOND. In other words, you take care of this life, and your wife takes care of the next one?

DAVENPORT. Objection.

JUDGE. Objection sustained.

DRUMMOND. Tell me, Mr. Sillers, while your wife was tending to the religion, did you ever happen to bump into a fella named Charles Darwin?

SILLERS. Not till recent.

DRUMMOND. Well, from what you've heard about this Darwin, do you think your wife would want to have him over for Sunday dinner? *(Drummond nudges Sillers with his elbow.)*

BRADY. *(Rising.)* Your Honor, my worthy opponent seems to me to be cluttering the issue with hypothetical questions —

DRUMMOND. I'm doing *your* job, Colonel.

DAVENPORT. *(Leaping up.)* The prosecution is perfectly able to handle its own arguments.

DRUMMOND. Look, I've just established that Mr. Sillers isn't working very hard at religion. Now, for your sake, I want to make sure he isn't working at evolution.

SILLERS. *(Simply)* I'm just working at the feed store.

DRUMMOND. *(To the Judge.)* This man's all right. *(Turning.)* Take a box seat, Mr. Sillers. *(Sillers starts toward the jury bench.)*

BRADY. I am not altogether satisfied that Mr. Sillers will render impartial judgement in this trial —

DRUMMOND. Out of order. The prosecution has already accepted this man. *(The following becomes a simultaneous wrangle among the attorneys.)*

BRADY. *(Moving to Drummond.)* I want a fair trial.

DRUMMOND. So do I!

BRADY. Unless the state of mind of the members of the jury conforms to the laws and patterns of society —

DRUMMOND. Conform! Conform! What do you want to do — run the jury through a meat-grinder, so they all come out the same?

DAVENPORT. *(Rising.)* Your Honor!

BRADY. I've seen what you can do to a jury. Twist and tangle them. Nobody's forgotten the Endicott Publishing case — where you made the jury believe the obscenity was in their own minds, not on the printed page. It was immoral what you did to that jury. Tricking them. Think you can get away with that here?

DRUMMOND. All I want is to prevent the clock-stoppers from dumping a load of medieval nonsense into the United States Constitution.

JUDGE. This is not a Federal court.

DRUMMOND. *(Slapping his hand on the table.)* Well, dammit, you've got to stop them somewhere. *(The crowd breaks out in disapproval. The Judge beats with his gavel.)*

JUDGE. Gentlemen, if you please, you are *both* out of order. The court rules that the jury has been selected. *(Brady lets his arms fall, and bows with benign acceptance, returning to his chair.)* Owing to the lateness of the hour and the unusual heat, the court will be recessed until ten o'clock tomorrow morning. *(Judge raps the gavel, rises, and the court rises and begins to break up. Then the Judge notices a slip of paper, and raps for order again.)* Oh. The Reverend Brown has asked me to announce that there will be a prayer meeting tonight on the courthouse lawn, to pray for justice and guidance. All are invited.

DRUMMOND. *(Rising.)* Your Honor. I object to this commercial announcement.

JUDGE. Commercial announcement?

DRUMMOND. For Reverend Brown's product. Why don't you announce that there will be an Evolutionist Meeting?

JUDGE. I have no knowledge of such a meeting.

DRUMMOND. That's understandable. It's bad enough that everybody coming into this courthouse has to walk underneath a banner that says "Read your Bible." Your Honor, I want that sign taken down. *(Crowd reaction of anger.)* Or else I want another one up. Just as big, just as big letters — saying, "Read your Darwin."

JUDGE. *(Furiously.)* Colonel Drummond, you are out of order. The court stands recessed. *(The Judge bangs his gavel, and fuming, leaves the bench. With the Judge's exit, the formality of a courtroom is relaxed. There is a feeling of relief as spectators and jurors adjust their sticky clothes, and start to move off, talking excitedly. All of the following, until Rachel rushes to Drummond, happens almost simultaneously to clear the courtroom. As spectators move out talking loudly, Mayor rushes to Brady.)*

MAYOR. Let me help you with your coat, Colonel Brady.

BRADY. Thank you, Mayor.

MAYOR. Exciting day, sir. *(Mrs. Blair and Dunlap lag behind exiting crowd.)*

DAVENPORT. I feel by and large it went well, don't you, Colonel?

BRADY. Fine, fine. Nothing to worry about. *(Hornbeck wanders off.)*

REUTERS REPORTER. Who'll be your first witness tomorrow, Colonel?

BRADY. You'll see.

MRS. BLAIR. *(Extends fan to Brady.)* Would you autograph my fan, Mr. Brady?

BRADY. Mrs. Brady has autograph cards.

DUNLAP. Bless you, Mr. Brady, for what you're doing. *(Mrs. Blair and Dunlap exit.)*

BROWN. *(Taking Mr. Brady's arm.)* You're coming to us for supper tonight, Colonel, in the Sunday School room, and afterwards, naturally, we'll expect you at our prayer meeting. *(They join Mrs. Brady, who has been waiting for her husband.)*

BRADY. Yes. Fine, excellent.

MRS. BRADY. They sent over some mail from the Mansion House. These letters will gladden your heart, Matt. *(Brady and his wife exit. Brown turns to Rachel, who has lagged behind waiting for a chance to talk to Cates.)*

BROWN. Rachel!

RACHEL. *(Not moving.)* Yes, Father. *(Brown exits.)*

MAYOR. *(To Davenport.)* I don't know if it's legal what I did about the "Colonel" business.

DAVENPORT. Don't worry. You won't get hit by a thunderbolt.

MAYOR. *(As he follows Davenport off.)* Sometimes I don't know — I just don't know. *(Noise of crowd exiting now fades out completely. All have gone except Rachel, Cates, Drummond and Meeker.)*

DRUMMOND. *(As he crosses to Meeker over the above.)* I don't think I have a correct copy of the indictment. *(Rachel moves to Cates.)*

MEEKER. Lemme see. *(Drummond hands Meeker indictment.)* Oh, you have the old one.

DRUMMOND. Well, let me have a new one.

MEEKER. Here. *(He gives Drummond a new indictment. Suddenly, Rachel darts to Drummond at Judge's bench. Cates opens his mouth to stop her, but she speaks rapidly, with pent-up tension.)*

RACHEL. Mr. Drummond. You've got to call the whole thing off. It's not too late. Bert knows he did wrong. He didn't mean to. And he's sorry. Now why can't he just stand up and say to everybody: "I did wrong. I broke the law. I admit it. I won't do it again." Then they'd stop all this fuss, and — everything would be like it was. *(Drummond looks at Rachel, not unkindly.)*

DRUMMOND. Who are you?

RACHEL. *(Backing down to Brady's table.)* I'm — a friend of Bert's.

35

DRUMMOND. How about it, boy? Getting cold feet?

CATES. I never thought it would be like this. Like Barnum and Bailey coming to town.

DRUMMOND. *(Easily.)* We can call it off. You want to quit?

RACHEL. Yes!

CATES. People look at me as if I was a murderer. Worse than a murderer! That fella from Minnesota who killed his wife — remember, Rache? — half the town turned out to watch 'em put him on the train. They just stared at him as if he was a curiosity — not like they *hated* him! Not like he'd done anything really wrong! Just different!

DRUMMOND. There's nothing very original about murdering your wife.

CATES. People I thought were my friends look at me now as if I had horns growing out of my head.

DRUMMOND. You murder a wife, it isn't nearly as bad as murdering an old wives' tale. Kill one of their fairy-tale notions, and they call down the wrath of God, Brady, and the state legislature.

RACHEL. You make a joke out of everything. You seem to think it's all so funny!

DRUMMOND. Lady, when you lose your power to laugh, you lose your power to think straight.

CATES. Mr. Drummond, I can't laugh. I'm scared.

DRUMMOND. Good. You'd be a damned fool if you weren't.

RACHEL. *(Bitterly.)* You're supposed to be helping Bert, and every time you swear you make it worse for him. *(She moves to Bert. He comforts her.)*

DRUMMOND. *(Honestly.)* I'm sorry if I offend you. But I don't swear just for the hell of it. You see, I figure that language is a poor enough means of communication as it is. So we ought to use all the words we've got. Besides, there are damned few words that everybody understands.

RACHEL. You don't care anything about Bert! You just want a chance to make speeches against the Bible!

DRUMMOND. I care a great deal about Bert. I care a great deal about what Bert thinks.

RACHEL. Well, I care about what the people in this town think of *him.*

36

DRUMMOND. *(Quietly.)* Can you buy back his respectability by making him a coward? *(He spades his hands in his hip pockets.)* I understand what Bert's going through. It's the loneliest feeling in the world — to find yourself standing up when everybody else is sitting down. To have everybody look at you and say, "What's the matter with him?" I know. I know what it feels like. Walking down an empty street, listening to the sound of your own footsteps. Shutters closed, blinds drawn, doors locked against you. And you aren't sure whether you're walking toward something — or just walking away ... *(He takes a deep breath, then turns abruptly.)* Cates, I'll change your plea and we'll call off the whole business — on one condition. If you honestly believe that you committed a criminal act against the citizens of this state and the minds of their children. If you honestly believe that you're wrong and the law's right. Then the hell with it. I'll pack my grip and go back to Chicago, where it's a cool hundred in the shade.

RACHEL. *(Eagerly.)* Bert knows he's wrong! Don't you, Bert?

DRUMMOND. Don't prompt the witness.

CATES. *(Going to Drummond.)* What do you think, Mr. Drummond?

DRUMMOND. I'm here. That tells you what I think. *(He looks squarely at Cates.)* Well, what's the verdict, Bert? You want to find yourself guilty before the jury does?

CATES. *(Quietly, with determination.)* No, sir. I'm not gonna quit.

RACHEL. *(Protesting.)* Bert — !

CATES. It wouldn't do any good now, anyhow. *(He turns to Rachel.)* If you'll stick by me, Rache — well, we can fight it out! *(He smiles at her wanly. Rachel shakes her head, bewildered, tears forming in her eyes.)*

RACHEL. *(Sinking into a chair.)* I don't know what to do; I don't know what to do — !

CATES. *(Crossing, half kneeling beside her.)* What's the matter, Rache?

RACHEL. I don't want to do it, Bert, but Mr. Brady says — I —

DRUMMOND. What does Mr. Brady say?

RACHEL. *(Looking down.)* They want me to testify against Bert!

CATES. *(Stunned.)* You can't — ! *(Meeker moves in a few steps.)*

37

MEEKER. Bert, I don't mean to rush you, but we gotta close up the shop. *(Cates is genuinely panicked — he moves automatically to Meeker, then runs back to kneel again beside Rachel.)*

CATES. Rache, some of the things I've talked to you about are things you just say to your own heart. If you get up on the stand and say those things out loud — *(He shakes his head.)* Don't you understand? The words I've said to you — softly, in the dark — just trying to figure out what the stars are for — or what might be on the back side of the moon —

MEEKER. Bert — *(Cates starts to go with Meeker, then turns again to Rachel.)*

CATES. They were questions, Rache: I was just asking questions! If you repeat those things on the witness stand, Brady'll make 'em sound like answers. And they'll crucify me! *(Meeker touches Bert's arm. Bert pulls away and almost runs off, followed more slowly by Meeker. Drummond crosses to Rachel who is in his chair. Takes his coat, puts it on, sizing up Rachel. Rachel, torn, is almost unconscious of his presence or of her surroundings.)*

DRUMMOND. *(Kindly, quietly.)* What's your name? Rachel what?

RACHEL. Rachel Brown. Can they make me testify?

DRUMMOND. I'm afraid so. It would be nice if nobody ever had to *make* anybody do anything. But — *(Takes his briefcase.)* Don't let Brady scare you. He only *seems* to be bigger than the law.

RACHEL. It's not Mr. Brady. It's my father.

DRUMMOND. Who's your father?

RACHEL. The Reverend Jeremiah Brown. *(Drummond whistles softly through his teeth.)* I used to feel this way when I was a little girl. I used to wake up at night, terrified of the dark. I'd think sometimes that my bed was on the ceiling, and the whole house was upside down; and if I didn't hang onto the mattress, I might fall outward into the stars. *(She shivers a little, remembering.)* I wanted to run to my father, and have him tell me I was safe, that everything was all right. But I was always more frightened of him than I was of falling. It's the same way now.

DRUMMOND. *(Softly.)* Is your mother dead?

RACHEL. I never knew my mother. *(Distraught.)* Is it true? Is Bert wicked?

DRUMMOND. *(With simple conviction.)* Bert Cates is a good man. Maybe even a great one. And it takes strength for a woman to love such a man. Especially when he's a pariah in the community .
RACHEL. I'm only confusing him. And he's confused enough as it is.
DRUMMOND. *(Takes his hat from under his chair.)* The man who has everything figured out is probably a fool. College examinations notwithstanding, it takes a very smart fella to say "I don't know the answer!" *(Drummond puts on his hat, touches the brim of it as a gesture of good-bye, and goes slowly off. The action is continuous as the lighting dissolves to the upper area.)*

Scene 3

The courthouse lawn. The same night. The oppressive heat of the day has softened into a pleasant summer evening.

Sillers and Dunlap, in work-clothes, are hammering at the makeshift platform, getting it ready for the prayer meeting. Sillers glances up at the "Read Your Bible" banner.

SILLERS. What're we gonna do about this sign?
DUNLAP. The devil don't run this town. Leave it up. *(Brady enters, followed by four reporters. Hornbeck brings up the rear, he alone is not bothering to take notes. Apparently this informal press conference has been in progress for some time, and Brady is now bringing it to a climax.)*
BRADY. — and I hope that you will tell the readers of your newspapers that here in Hillsboro we are fighting the fight of the Faithful throughout the world! *(All write. Brady eyes Hornbeck, leaning lazily, not writing.)*
REUTERS MAN. *(British accent.)* A question, Mr. Brady.
BRADY. Certainly. Where are you from, young man?
REPORTER. London, sir. Reuters News Agency. *(NOTE:*

Pronounced "Royters." The sound of people humming softly the hymn, "Revive Us Again" as they gather.)

BRADY. Excellent. I have many friends in the United Kingdom.

REUTERS MAN. What is your personal opinion of Henry Drummond?

BRADY. I'm glad you asked me that. I want people everywhere to know I bear no personal animosity toward Henry Drummond. There was a time when we were on the same side of the fence. He gave me active support in my campaign in 1908 — and I welcomed it. *(Almost impassioned, speaking at writing tempo, so all the reporters can get it down.)* But I say that if my own *brother* challenged the faith of millions, as Mr. Drummond is doing, I would oppose him still! *(Dunlap pounds.)* I think that's all for this evening, gentlemen. *(The reporters move in a knot of discussion. Brady crosses to Hornbeck.)* Mr. Hornbeck, my clipping service has sent me some of your dispatches. *(Humming quietly, the townspeople continue to gather.)*

HORNBECK. How flattering to know I'm being clipped.

BRADY. It grieves me to read reporting that is so — biased.

HORNBECK. I'm no reporter, Colonel. I'm a critic.

BRADY. I hope you will stay for Reverend Brown's prayer meeting. It may bring you some enlightenment.

HORNBECK. It may. I'm here on a press pass, and I don't intend to miss any part of the show. *(Rev. Brown enters, Mrs. Brady on his arm. Hornbeck passes them jauntily, leans against a hitching-post to watch.)*

BRADY. Good evening, Reverend. How are you, Mother?

MRS. BRADY. The Reverend Brown was good enough to escort me.

BRADY. Reverend, I'm looking forward to your prayer meeting.

BROWN. You will find our people are fervent in their belief. *(Mrs. Brady turns to her husband.)*

MRS. BRADY. I know it's warm, Matt; but these night breezes can be treacherous. And you know how you perspire. *(She takes a small kerchief out of her handbag and tucks it around his neck. He laughs a little.)*

BRADY. Mother is always so worried about my throat.

BROWN. *(Consulting his watch.)* I always like to begin my meetings at the time announced.

BRADY. Most commendable. Proceed, Reverend. After you. *(Brown mounts the few steps to the platform. Brady follows him, loving the feel of the board beneath his feet. This is the squared circle where he has fought so many bouts with the English language, and won. As the Reverend and Brady mount the platform the townspeople, still humming, take their places for the prayer meeting. All focus on Reverend on platform. The prayer meeting is motion picture, radio, and tent show to these people. To them, the Reverend Brown is a combination Milton Sills and Douglas Fairbanks. He grasps the railing and stares down at them sternly. Brady is benign. He sits with his legs crossed, an arm crooked over one corner of his chair. Brown is milking the expectant pause. Just as he is ready to speak, Drummond comes in, stands at the fringe of the crowd. Brown glares at Drummond. The crowd is still humming.)*

BROWN. Brothers and sisters, I come to you on the Wings of the Word. The Wings of the Word are beating loud in the treetops! The Lord's Word is howling in the Wind, and flashing in the belly of the Cloud!

MRS. KREBS. I hear it!

ELIJAH. I see it, Reverend!

BROWN. And we *believe* the Word!

ALL. We believe!

BROWN. We believe the Glory of the Word!

ALL. Glory, Glory! Amen, amen! *(Rachel enters. The townspeople have heard the Reverend tell this story countless times, and they love it. They have familiar responses, which they make — with minor variations — with Brown's narration providing the solo melody, and the answers of the townspeople forming a well-orchestrated counterpoint. The tone at the beginning is subdued, almost pastoral, but the voices and faces contain the seed of the frenzy which will burst forth later on.)*

BROWN. Hearken to the Word! *(He lowers his voice.)* The Word tells us that the World was created in Seven Days.

ALL. Amen.

BROWN. In the beginning, the earth was without form, and void. And the Lord said, "Let there be light!" And there *was* light!

ALL. Praise the Lord. *(The humming now stops completely.)*

BROWN. And the Lord saw the Light and the Light saw the Lord, and the Light said, "Am I good, Lord?" And the Lord said,

41

"Thou art good!"

ELIJAH. *(Deep-voiced, singing.)* And the evening and the morning were the first day!

VOICES. Amen, amen!

BROWN. *(Calling out.)* The Lord said, "Let there be Firmament!" And even as He spoke, it was so! And the Firmament bowed down before Him and said, "Am I good, Lord?" And the Lord said, "Thou art good!"

ELIJAH. *(Singing.)* And the evening and the morning were the second day!

VOICES. Amen, amen!

BROWN. *(With mounting tempo.)* On the Third day brought He forth the Dry Land, and the Grass, and the Fruit Tree! And on the Fourth Day made He the Sun, the Moon, and the Stars — and He pronounced them Good!

VOICES. Amen.

BROWN. On the Fifth Day He peopled the sea with fish. And the air with fowl. And made He great whales.

MRS. LOOMIS. Hallelujah!

BROWN. And He blessed them all. *(Pauses, then gravely.)* But on the morning of the Sixth Day, the Lord rose, and His eye was dark and a scowl lay across His face. *(Shouts.)* Why?

ALL. Why?

BROWN. Why was the Lord troubled?

ALL. Why? Tell us why! Tell us the troubles of the Lord!

BROWN. *(Dropping his voice almost to a whisper.)* He looked about Him, did the Lord; at all His handiwork, bowed down before Him. And He said, "It is not good — "

ALL. *(Moan.)* Oh.

BROWN. It is not enough — "

ALL. *(Moan.)* Oh.

BROWN. It is not finished.

ALL. *(Moan.)* Oh, Lord!

BROWN. I ... shall ... make ... Me ... a ... *Man!*" *(The crowd bursts out into an orgy of hosannahs and waving arms.)*

ALL. Glory! Hosannah! Bless the Lord who created us!

MRS. KREBS. *(Throwing herself to the ground. Shouting out.)* Bow down! Bow down before the Lord!

ELIJAH. Are we good, Lord? Tell us! Are we good?

BROWN. *(Answering triumphantly.)* The Lord said, "Yea, thou art good! For I have created ye in My Image, after My Likeness! Be fruitful, and multiply, and replenish the Earth, and subdue it!"

ELIJAH. *(Deep-voiced, singing.)* The Lord made Man master of the Earth...!

ALL. Glory, glory! Bless the Lord!

BROWN. *(Whipping 'em up.)* Do we believe?

ALL. *(In chorus.)* Yes!

BROWN. Do we believe the Word?

ALL. *(Coming back like a whip-crack.)* Yes!

BROWN. Do we believe the Truth of the Word?

ALL. Yes!

BROWN. *(Pointing a finger toward the jail.)* Do we curse the man who denies the Word?

ALL. *(Crescendo, each answer mightier than the one before.)* Yes!

BROWN. Do we cast out this sinner in our midst?

ALL. Yes! *(Each crash of sound from the crowd seems to strike Rachel physically, and shake her. The prayer meeting has passed beyond the familiar bounds into an area of orgiastic anger.)*

BROWN. Do we call down hellfire on the man who has sinned against the Word?

ALL. *(Roaring.)* Yes!

BROWN. *(Deliberately shattering the rhythm, to go into a frenzied prayer, hands clasped together and lifted heavenward.)* O Lord of the Tempest and the Thunder! O Lord of Righteousness and Wrath! We pray that Thou wilt make a sign unto us! Strike down this sinner, as Thou didst Thine enemies of old, in the days of the Pharaohs! *(All lean forward, almost expecting the heavens to open with a thunderbolt. Rachel is white. Brady shifts uncomfortably in his chair, this is pretty strong stuff, even for him.)* Let him feel the terror of Thy sword! For all eternity, let his soul writhe in anguish and damnation —

RACHEL. *No! (She rushes to the platform.)* No, Father. Don't pray to destroy Bert! *(As she falls to her knees in front of the platform.)* No, no, no...!

BROWN. Lord, we call down the same curse on those who ask grace for this sinner — though they be blood of my blood, and

43

flesh of my flesh!

BRADY. *(Rising, grasping Brown's arm.)* Reverend Brown, I know it is the great zeal of your faith which makes you utter this prayer! But it is possible to be *over*zealous, to destroy that which you hope to save — so that nothing is left but emptiness. *(Brown turns.)* Remember the wisdom of Solomon in the Book of Proverbs — *(Softly.)* "He that troubleth his own house ... shall inherit the wind." *(He makes a gesture with his open hand to indicate nothingness: the empty air, the brief and unremembered wind. Brady leads Brown to chair on platform and sits him down. Brown seems dazed, shaken. Benignly, Brady turns to the townspeople.)* The Bible also tells us that God forgives His children. And we, the Children of God, should forgive each other. *(Rachel slips off.)* My good friends, return to your homes. The blessings of the Lord be with you all. *(Slowly the townspeople move off, singing and humming "Go, Tell It On the Mountain." When the crowd has almost cleared, Rev. Brown steps off platform to Mrs. Brady. Brady moves off platform, motions them off. Brady and Drummond are left alone on stage. As Brady crosses to Drummond.)* We were good friends once. I was always glad of your support. What happened between us? There used to be a mutuality of understanding and admiration. Why is it, my old friend, that you have moved so far away from me? *(A pause. They study each other.)*

DRUMMOND. *(Slowly.)* All motion is relative. Perhaps it is *you* who have moved away — by standing still. *(The words have a sharp impact on Brady. For a moment, he stands still, his mouth open, staring at Drummond. Then he takes two faltering steps backward, looks at Drummond again, then moves off. Drummond stands alone. Slowly the lights fade on the silent man.)*

Curtain

End of Act One

ACT TWO

Scene 1

The courtroom, two days later.

Again, out of the darkness, the lights bump up to a golden portrait, frozen in time: bright midday, the trial in full swing.

The action starts, the fans pump. The Judge is on the bench; the jury, lawyers, officials and spectators crowd the courtroom.

Three witnesses are seated in the front row among the spectators: the scientists Aaronson, Keller, and Page. Aaronson is Einstein-like. Page holds a specimen box in his lap (later we will see that it contains a rock which splits to reveal a fossil). The schoolboy Howard is on the witness stand. He is wretched in a starched collar and Sunday suit. The weather is as relentlessly hot as before. Brady is examining the boy, who is a witness for the prosecution.

BRADY. Go on, Howard. Tell them what else Mr. Cates told you in the classroom.
HOWARD. Well, he said at first the earth was too hot for any life. Then it cooled off a mite, and cells and things begun to live.
BRADY. Cells?
HOWARD. Little bugs, like, in the water. After that, the little bugs got to be bigger bugs, and sprouted legs and crawled up on the land.
BRADY. How long did this take, according to Mr. Cates?
HOWARD. Couple million years. Maybe longer. Then comes the fishes and the reptiles and the mammals. Man's a mammal.

45

BRADY. Along with the dogs and the cattle in the field: did he say that?

HOWARD. Yes, sir. *(Drummond is about to protest against prompting the witness, then he decides it isn't worth the trouble.)*

BRADY. Now, Howard, how did *man* come out of this slimy, mess of bugs and serpents, according to your — "Professor"?

HOWARD. Man was sort of evoluted. From the "Old World Monkeys." *(Brady slaps his thigh.)*

BRADY. *(Crossing to jury.)* Did you hear that, my friends? "Old World Monkeys"! According to Mr. Cates, you and I aren't even descended from good American monkeys! *(There is laughter from spectators. Brady turns back to Howard.)* Howard, listen carefully. In all this talk of bugs and "Evil-ution," of slime and ooze, did Mr. Cates ever make any reference to God?

HOWARD. Not as I remember.

BRADY. Or the miracle He achieved in seven days as described in the beautiful Book of Genesis?

HOWARD. No, sir. *(Brady stretches out his arms in an all-embracing gesture.)*

BRADY. Ladies and gentlemen —

DRUMMOND. Objection! *(Rising.)* I ask that the court remind the learned counsel that this is not a Chautauqua tent. He is supposed to be submitting evidence to a jury. There are no ladies on the jury. *(He sits. There is a low mutter from the spectators.)*

BRADY. Your Honor, I have no intention of making a speech. There is no need. I am sure that everyone on the jury, everyone within the sound of this boy's voice, is moved by this tragic confusion. He has been taught that he wriggled up like an animal from the filth and the muck below! *(Continuing fervently, the spirit is upon him.)* I say that the Bible-haters, these "Evil-utionists," are brewers of poison! And the legislature of this sovereign state has had the wisdom to demand that the peddlers of poison — in bottles — *(Turns and points to Cates.)* or in books — clearly label the products they attempt to sell! *(There is an applause from the spectators. Howard gulps. Brady points at the boy.)* I tell you, if this law is not upheld, this boy will become one of a generation, shorn of its faith by the teachings of Godless science! But if the full penalty of the law is meted out to Bertram Cates, the faithful the whole world over, who are watching us here, and listening to our every word, will call this courtroom blessed! *(Applause from the spectators. Even one of the jury members is moved to applaud, but is stopped by his neighbors. Dramatically, Brady moves to his chair. Condescendingly, he waves to Drummond.)* Your witness, sir. *(Brady sits. Drummond rises, slouches toward the witness stand.)*

DRUMMOND. Well, I sure am glad Colonel Brady didn't make a speech! *(Nobody laughs. The courtroom seems to resent Drummond's gentle ridicule of the orator. To many, there is an effrontery in Drummond's very voice — folksy and relaxed. It's rather like a harmonica following a symphony concert.)* Howard, I heard you say that the world used to be pretty hot.

HOWARD. That's what Mr. Cates said.

DRUMMOND. You figure it was any hotter then than it is right now?

HOWARD. Guess it musta been. Mr. Cates read it to us from a book.

DRUMMOND. Do you know what book?

HOWARD. I guess that Mr. Darwin thought it up.

DRUMMOND. *(Leaning on the arm of the boy's chair.)* You figure anything's wrong with that, Howard?

HOWARD. Well, I dunno —

DAVENPORT. *(Leaping up, crisply.)* Objection, Your Honor. The defense is asking that a thirteen-year-old boy hand down an opinion on a question of morality!

DRUMMOND. *(To the judge.)* I am trying to establish, Your Honor, that Howard — or Colonel Brady — or Charles Darwin — or anyone in this courtroom — or *you*, sir — has the right to *think!*

JUDGE. Colonel Drummond, the right to think is not on trial here.

DRUMMOND. *(Energetically.)* With all respect to the bench. I hold that the right to think is very much on trial! It is fearfully in danger in the proceedings of this court!

BRADY. *(Rises.)* A *man* is on trial!

DRUMMOND. A *thinking* man! And he is threatened with fine and imprisonment because he chooses to speak what he thinks.

JUDGE. Colonel Drummond, would you please rephrase your question. *(Brady returns to his table, sits. Drummond crosses to Howard.)*

47

DRUMMOND. Let's put it this way, Howard. All this fuss and feathers about Evolution, do you think it hurt you any?

HOWARD. Sir?

DRUMMOND. Did it do you any harm? You still feel reasonably fit? What Mr. Cates told you, did it hurt your baseball game any? Affect your pitching arm? *(He punches Howard's right arm playfully.)*

HOWARD. No, sir. I'm a leftie.

DRUMMOND. A southpaw, eh? Still honor your father and mother?

HOWARD. Sure.

DRUMMOND. Haven't murdered anybody since breakfast? *(Low murmur from the spectators.)*

DAVENPORT. Objection.

JUDGE. Objection sustained. *(Drummond shrugs.)*

BRADY. *(Jumps up.)* Ask him if his Holy Faith in the scriptures has been shattered —

DRUMMOND. When I need your *valuable* help, Colonel, you may rest assured I shall humbly ask for it. *(Brady returns to his chair. Drummond turns back to the boy in a pleasantly familiar manner.)* Howard, do you believe everything Mr. Cates told you?

HOWARD. *(Frowning.)* I'm not sure. I gotta think it over.

DRUMMOND. Good for you. Your pa's a farmer, isn't he?

HOWARD. Yes, sir.

DRUMMOND. Got a tractor?

HOWARD. Brand new one.

DRUMMOND. You figure a tractor's sinful, because it isn't mentioned in the Bible?

HOWARD. *(Thinking.)* Don't know.

DRUMMOND. Moses never made a phone call. Suppose that makes the telephone an instrument of the Devil?

HOWARD. I never thought of it that way.

BRADY. *(Rising, booming.)* Neither did anybody else! Your Honor, the defense makes the same old error of all Godless men! They confuse material things with the great spiritual realities of the Revealed Word! *(Turning to Drummond.)* Why do you bewilder this child? Does Right have no meaning to you, sir? *(Brady's hands are outstretched, palms upward, pleading. Drummond stares*

48

at Brady long and thoughtfully.)

DRUMMOND. Realizing that I may prejudice the case of my client, I must say that "Right" has no meaning to me whatsoever! *(There is buzz of reaction in the courtroom.)* Truth has meaning — as a direction. But one of the peculiar imbecilities of our time is the grid of morality we have placed on human behavior: so that every act of man must be measured against an arbitrary latitude of degrees! *(He looks from Juror to Juror. The faces stare back blankly; he might as well be speaking Chinese. Drummond turns back to Howard.)* Do *you* have any idea what I'm talking about, Howard?

HOWARD. No, sir.

DRUMMOND. Well, maybe you will. Some day. Thank you, son. That's all. *(Pleasantly, Drummond musses the boy's hair, then crosses back to his chair and sits.)*

JUDGE. The witness is excused. *(He raps his gavel, but Howard remains in the chair, staring goop-eyed at his newly found idol. There is a low murmur of mixed amusement and indignation.)* We won't need you any more, Howard: you can go back to your pa now. *(Two raps from the Judge's gavel bring Howard back to reality. He rises, runs to his seat — pausing to grin at Drummond, who smiles back.)* Next witness.

DAVENPORT. Will Miss Rachel Brown come forward, please? *(Low murmur from spectators. Rachel rises unsteadily and crosses to witness stand. She moves quickly, as if wanting the whole thing over with. She looks at no one. Cates watches her with a hopeless expression: Et tu, Brute. Meeker swears her in perfunctorily. She sits. Brady crosses to her.)*

BRADY. Miss Brown. You are a teacher at the Hillsboro Consolidated School?

RACHEL. Yes.

BRADY. So you have had ample opportunity to know the defendant, Mr. Cates, professionally?

RACHEL. Yes.

BRADY. *(With exaggerated gentleness.)* Is Mr. Cates a member of the spiritual community to which you belong?

DRUMMOND. *(Rises.)* Objection! I don't understand this chatter about "spiritual communities." If the prosecution wants to know if they go to the same church, why doesn't he ask that?

JUDGE. Uh — objection overruled. *(Drummond slouches, dis-gruntled. Cates stares at Rachel disbelievingly, while her eyes remain on the floor. The exchange between Drummond and the Judge seems to have unnerved her, however.)* You will answer the question, please.

RACHEL. *(Confused.)* I did answer it, didn't I? What was the question?

BRADY. Do you and Mr. Cates attend the same church? *(There are satisfied chuckles from the townspeople at this minor magnanimity.)*

RACHEL. Not any more. Bert dropped out two summers ago.

BRADY. Why?

RACHEL. It was what happened with the little Stebbins boy.

BRADY. Would you tell us about that, please?

RACHEL. The boy was eleven years old, and he went swimming in the river, and got a cramp and drowned. Bert felt awful about it. He lived right next door, and Tommy Stebbins used to come over to the boarding house and look though Bert's microscope. Bert said the boy had a quick mind, and he might even be a sci-entist when he grew up. At the funeral, Pa preached that Tommy didn't die in a state of grace, because his folks had never had him baptized — *(Cates, who has been smoldering through this citation, suddenly leaps angrily to his feet.)*

CATES. Tell 'em what your father really said! That Tommy's soul was damned, writhing in hellfire!

DUNLAP. *(Jumping up and shaking a fist at Cates.)* Cates, you sinner! *(The Judge raps for order. Finney jumps up, holds Dunlap back. The spectators are vehement in their disapproval of Cates. But the scientists — Aaronson, Keller, and Page — sit in quiet embar-rassment. There is confusion in the courtroom.)*

CATES. Religion's supposed to comfort people, isn't it? Not frighten them to death!

JUDGE. *(Pounding gavel loudly.)* We will have order, please! *(The commotion subsides. Drummond tugs Cates back to his seat.)*

DRUMMOND. *(Rises.)* Your Honor, I request that the defendant's remarks be stricken from the record. *(He sits. The Judge nods.)*

BRADY. But how can we strike this young man's bigoted opin-ions from the memory of this community? *(Brady turns, about to play his trump card.)* Now, my dear. Will you tell the jury some more of Mr. Cates' opinions on the subject of religion?

DRUMMOND. *(Leaps up.)* Objection! Objection! Objection! Hearsay testimony is not admissible.

JUDGE. The court sees no objection to this line of questioning. Proceed, Colonel Brady. *(Drummond sinks back, disgusted.)*

BRADY. Will you merely repeat in your words some of the conversations you had with the defendant? *(Rachel's eyes meet Bert's. She hesitates.)*

RACHEL. I don't remember exactly —

BRADY. *(Helpfully.)* What you told me the other day. That presumably "humorous" remark Mr. Cates made about the Heavenly Father. *(Low gasps of outrage from spectators.)*

RACHEL. Bert said — *(She stops.)*

BRADY. Go ahead, my dear.

RACHEL. *(Pathetically.)* I can't — *(Brady looks to the Judge. Reverend Brown rises, stands in his place, glowering at his daughter.)*

JUDGE. May I remind you, Miss Brown, that you are testifying under oath, and it is unlawful to withhold pertinent information.

RACHEL. Bert was just talking about some of the things he'd read. He — he — *(Rev. Brown sits slowly.)*

BRADY. Were you shocked when he told you these things? *(Rachel looks down.)* Describe to the court your innermost feelings when Bertram Cates said to you: "God did not create Man! Man created God!" *(There is a flurry of reaction. Loud outrage from the spectators. Judge gavels for quiet.)*

DRUMMOND. *(Leaping to his feet.)* Objection!

RACHEL. *(Rises, topping the spectators.)* Bert didn't say that! He was just joking. What he said was: *(Spectators quiet.)* "God created Man in His own image — and Man, being a gentleman, returned the compliment." *(Hornbeck guffaws and pointedly scribbles this down. Another outburst from the spectators. Judge gavels them quiet. Drummond sits throwing a wry smile at Cates. Brady is pleased. Rachel seems hopelessly torn.)*

BRADY. Go on, my dear. Tell us some more. What did he say about the holy state of matrimony? Did he compare it with the breeding of animals?

RACHEL. No, he didn't say that — He didn't *mean* that. That's not what I told you. All he said was — *(She opens her mouth to speak, but nothing comes out. An emotional block makes her unable to utter a sound. Her lips move wordlessly.)*

JUDGE. Are you ill, Miss Brown? Would you care for a glass of water? *(Meeker crosses, gets water glass from Judge's table, passes it to Brady who offers it to Rachel. She refuses it. She seems on the brink of collapse.)*

BRADY. Under the circumstances, I believe the witness should be dismissed.

DRUMMOND. *(Rises.)* And will the defense have no chance to challenge some of these statements the prosecutor has put in the mouth of the witness? *(Cates is moved by Rachel's obvious distress.)*

CATES. *(To Drummond.)* Don't plague her. Let her go.

DRUMMOND. *(Pauses, then sighs.)* No questions. *(Sits.)*

JUDGE. For the time being, the witness is excused. *(Reverend Brown comes forward to help his daughter from the stand, he escorts her from the courtroom. There is a hushed babble of excitement.)* Does the prosecution wish to call any further witnesses?

DAVENPORT. Not at the present time, Your Honor.

JUDGE. We shall proceed with the case for the defense. Colonel Drummond. *(Spectators whisper briefly.)*

DRUMMOND. *(Rising, searches with his eyes for Dr. Keller, finds him.)* Your Honor, I wish to call Dr. Amos D. Keller, *(Keller rises.)* head of the Department of Zoology at the University of Chicago. *(Keller steps forward.)*

BRADY. Objection. *(Drummond turns, startled.)*

DRUMMOND. On what grounds?

BRADY. *(Rising.)* I wish to inquire what possible relevance the testimony of a *Zoo*-ology professor can have in this trial.

DRUMMOND. *(Reasonably.)* It has every relevance! My client is on trial for teaching Evolution. Any testimony relating to his alleged infringement of the law must be admitted!

BRADY. Irrelevant, immaterial, inadmissible. *(Brady sits.)*

DRUMMOND. *(Sharply.)* Why? *(To the Judge.)* If Bertram Cates were accused of murder, would it be irrelevant to call expert witnesses to examine the weapon? Would you rule out testimony that the so-called murder weapon was incapable of firing a bullet?

JUDGE. *(Hesitantly.)* I fail to grasp the learned counsel's meaning.

DRUMMOND. Oh. *(With exaggerated gestures, as if explaining things to a small child.)* Your Honor, the defense wishes to place Dr. Keller on the witness stand, so that he may explain to the gentlemen of the jury exactly what the evolutionary theory is. *(Turning to Judge, who is indignant.)* How can they pass judgement on it if they don't know what it's all about?

BRADY. *(Rises.)* I hold that the very law we are here to enforce excludes such testimony! The people of this state have made it very clear that they do not want this *zoo*-ological hogwash slobbered around the schoolrooms! *(Medium low reaction of approval from spectators.)* And I refuse to allow these agnostic scientists to employ this courtroom as a sounding board, as a platform from which they can shout their heresies into the headlines! *(Spectators applaud.)*

JUDGE. *(After some thoughtful hesitation.)* Colonel Drummond, the court rules that zoology is irrelevant to the case. *(The Judge flashes his customary mechanical and humorless grin. Puzzled, Keller sits.)*

DRUMMOND. Agnostic scientists! *(Crossing to Brady.)* Then I call Dr. Allen Page — *(Page rises. Drummond stares straight at Brady.)* Deacon of the Congregational Church — and professor of geology and archeology at Oberlin College.

BRADY. *(Dryly.)* Objection!

JUDGE. Objection sustained. *(Again, the meaningless grin. Page sits.)*

DRUMMOND. *(Astonished.)* In one breath, does the court deny the existence of zoology, geology and archeology?

JUDGE. We do not deny the existence of these sciences: but they do not relate to this point of law.

DRUMMOND. *(Fiery.)* I call Walter Aaronson, *(Aaronson rises.)* philosopher, anthropologist, author! One of the most brilliant minds in the world today! *(Turns to Brady.)* Objection, Colonel Brady?

BRADY. *(Nodding, smugly.)* Objection. *(Aaronson sits.)*

DRUMMOND. *(Intensely.)* Your Honor! The Defense has brought to Hillsboro — at great expense and inconvenience — fifteen noted scientists! The great thinkers of our time! Their testimony is basic to the defense of my client. For it is my intent to show this court that what Bertram Cates spoke quietly one spring afternoon

53

in the Hillsboro High School is no crime! It is incontrovertible as geometry in every enlightened community of minds!

JUDGE. In *this* community, Colonel Drummond — and in this sovereign state — exactly the opposite is the case. The language of the law is clear; we do not need experts to question the validity of a law that is already on the books. *(Drummond, for once in his life, has hit a legal roadblock.)*

DRUMMOND. *(Scowling.)* In other words, the court rules out any expert testimony on Charles Darwin's *Origin of Species* or *Descent of Man*?

JUDGE. The court so rules. *(Drummond is flabbergasted. His case is cooked and he knows it. He looks around helplessly. He strides angrily to his table and starts to pack his briefcase. As he crosses, spectators whisper excitedly at the turn of events. Drummond suddenly stops packing.)*

DRUMMOND. *(There's the glint of an idea in his eye.)* Would the court admit expert testimony regarding a book known as the Holy Bible?

JUDGE. *(Hesitates, turns to Brady.)* Any objection, Colonel Brady?

BRADY. If the counsel can advance the case of the defendant through the use of the Holy Scriptures, the prosecution will take no exception!

DRUMMOND. Good! *(With relish.)* I call to the stand one of the world's foremost experts on the Bible and its teachings — *(Brady and all turn, trying to see who Drummond's "surprise witness" may be.)* Matthew Harrison Brady! *(There is an uproar in the courtroom. The Judge raps for order. Brady is stunned.)*

DAVENPORT. *(Rises.)* Your Honor, this is preposterous!

JUDGE. *(Confused.)* I — well, it's highly unorthodox. I've never known an instance where the defense called the prosecuting attorney as a witness. *(Brady rises.)*

BRADY. Your Honor, this entire trial is unorthodox. If the interests of Right and Justice will be served, I will take the stand.

DAVENPORT. *(Helplessly.)* But, Colonel Brady — *(Buzz of awed reaction. The giants are about to meet head on. The Judge raps the gavel again, nervously.)*

JUDGE. *(To Brady.)* The court will support you if you wish to decline to testify — as a witness against your own case ...

BRADY. *(With conviction.)* Your Honor, I shall not testify *against* anything. I shall speak out, as I have all my life — on behalf of the Living Truth of the Holy Scriptures! *(Medium loud "Amens" and applause from the spectators. Davenport sits, resigned but nervous.)*

JUDGE. *(To Meeker, in a nervous whisper.)* Uh — Mr. Meeker, you'd better swear in the witness, please ... *(Drummond moistens his lips in anticipation. Brady moves to the witness stand in grandiose style. Meeker holds out a Bible. Brady puts his left hand on the book, and raises his right hand.)*

MEEKER. Do you solemnly swear to tell the truth, the whole truth, and nothing but the truth, so help you God?

BRADY. *(Booming.)* I do.

MRS. KREBS. And he will! *(Spectators agree. Brady sits, confident and assured. His air is that of a benign and learned mathematician about to be quizzed by a schoolboy on matters of short division.)*

DRUMMOND. Am I correct, sir, in calling on you as an authority on the Bible?

BRADY. I believe it is not boastful to say that I have studied the Bible as much as any layman. And I have tried to live according to its precepts.

DRUMMOND. Bully for you. Now, I suppose you can quote me chapter and verse right straight through the King James Version, can't you?

BRADY. There are many portions of the Holy Bible that I have committed to memory. *(Drummond crosses to counsel table and picks up a copy of Darwin.)*

DRUMMOND. I don't suppose you've memorized many passages from *The Origin of Species*? *(Davenport tries to get the Judge's attention.)*

BRADY. I am not in the least interested in the pagan hypotheses of that book.

DRUMMOND. Never read it?

BRADY. And I never will.

DRUMMOND. Then how in perdition do you have the gall to whoop up this holy war against something you don't know anything about? How can you be so cocksure that the body of scientific knowledge systematized in the writings of Charles

Darwin is, in any way, irreconcilable with the spirit of the Book of Genesis?

BRADY. Would you state that question again, please? *(Spectators laugh.)*

DRUMMOND. Let me put it this way. *(He flips several pages in the book.)* On page nineteen of *Origin of Species*, Darwin states — *(Davenport leaps up.)*

DAVENPORT. I object to this, Your Honor. Colonel Brady has been called as an authority on the Bible. Now the "gentleman from Chicago" is using this opportunity to read into the record scientific testimony which you, Your Honor, have previously ruled is irrelevant. If he's going to examine Colonel Brady on the Bible, let him stick to the Bible, the Holy Bible, and only the Bible! *(Approval with amens and applause from the spectators. Drummond cocks an eye at the bench.)*

JUDGE. *(Clears his throat.)* You will confine your questions to the Bible. *(Davenport sits smugly. Drummond slaps shut the volume of Darwin.)*

DRUMMOND. *(Not angrily, crossing to his table.)* All right. I get the scent in the wind. *(He tosses the volume of Darwin on the counsel table.)* We'll play in *your* ball park, Colonel. *(He searches for a copy of the Bible, finally gets Meeker's. Without opening it Drummond scrutinizes the binding from several angles.)* Now let's get this straight. Let's get it clear. This *is* the book that you're an expert on? *(Brady is annoyed at Drummond's elementary attitude and condescension.)*

BRADY. That is correct.

DRUMMOND. Now tell me. Do you feel that every word that's written in this book should be taken literally?

BRADY. Everything in the Bible should be accepted, exactly as it is given there. *(Medium loud "amens" from the spectators. Drummond looks askance toward the "amen" corner.)*

DRUMMOND. *(Leafing through the Bible.)* Now take this place where the whale swallows Jonah. Do you figure that actually happened?

BRADY. The Bible does not say "a whale," it says "a big fish." *(Low snicker from spectators.)*

DRUMMOND. *(Finds the place in the Bible, shows it to Brady.)*

Matter of fact, it says " a great fish" — but it's pretty much the same thing. What's your feeling about that?

BRADY. I believe in a God who can make a whale and who can make a man and make both do what He pleases!

SPECTATORS. *(Loudly.)* Amen, amen!

DRUMMOND. *(Turning sharply to the Court Recorder.)* I want those "Amens" in the record! *(He wheels back to Brady.)* I recollect a story about Joshua, making the sun stand still. Now as an expert, you tell me that's as true as the Jonah business. Right? *(Brady nods, blandly.)* That's a pretty neat trick. You suppose Houdini could do it?

BRADY. I do not question or scoff at the miracles of the Lord — as do ye of little faith.

DRUMMOND. Have you ever pondered just what would naturally happen to the earth if the sun stood still?

BRADY. You can testify to that if I get you on the stand. *(There is laughter from the spectators.)*

DRUMMOND. If they say that the sun stood still, they must've had a notion that the sun moves around the earth. Think that's the way of things? Or don't you believe the earth moves around the sun?

BRADY. I have faith in the Bible!

DRUMMOND. You don't have much faith in the solar system.

BRADY. *(Doggedly.)* The sun stopped.

DRUMMOND. Good. *(Dramatizing it.)* Now if what you say factually happened — if Joshua halted the sun in the sky — that means the earth stopped spinning on its axis; continents toppled over each other, mountains flew out into space. And the earth, arrested in its orbit, shriveled to a cinder and crashed into the sun. How come they missed *this* tidbit of news?

BRADY. They missed it because it didn't happen.

DRUMMOND. It must've happened! According to natural law. Or don't you believe in natural law, Colonel? Would you like to ban Copernicus from the classroom, along with Charles Darwin? Pass a law to wipe out all the scientific development since Joshua. Revelations — period!

BRADY. *(Calmly, as if instructing a child.)* Natural law was born in the mind of the Heavenly Father. He can change it, cancel it, use it as He pleases. It constantly amazes me that you apostles of science for all your supposed wisdom, fail to grasp this simple fact.

(Low brief buzz from spectators. Drummond, shaking his head flips a few pages in the Bible.)

DRUMMOND. Listen to this: Genesis 4-16. "And Cain went out from the presence of the Lord, and dwelt in the land of Nod, on the East of Eden. And Cain *knew his wife!*" Where the hell did *she* come from?

BRADY. Who?

DRUMMOND. Mrs. Cain. Cain's wife. If, "In the beginning" there were only Adam and Eve, and Cain and Abel, where'd this extra woman spring from? Ever figure that out?

BRADY. *(Cool.)* No, sir. I will leave the agnostics to hunt for her. *(Laughter from the spectators.)*

DRUMMOND. Never bothered you?

BRADY. Never bothered me.

DRUMMOND. Never tried to find out?

BRADY. No.

DRUMMOND. Figure somebody pulled off another creation, over in the next county?

BRADY. The Bible satisfies me, it is enough.

DRUMMOND. It frightens me to imagine the state of learning in this world if everyone had your driving curiosity. *(Drummond is still probing for a weakness in Goliath's armor. He thumbs a few pages further in the Bible.)* This book now goes into a lot of "begats." *(He reads.)* "And Aphraxad begat Salah; and Salah begat Eber" and so on and so on. *(Turning to Brady.)* These pretty important folks?

BRADY. They are the generations of the holy men and women of the Bible.

DRUMMOND. How did they go about all this "begatting"?

BRADY. What do you mean?

DRUMMOND. I mean, did people "begat" in those days about the same way they get themselves "begat" today?

BRADY. The process is about the same. I don't think your scientists have improved it any.

DRUMMOND. In other words, these folks were conceived and brought forth through the normal biological function known as *sex. (Gasps of shock, and a sputter of hush-hush reaction through the court. Howard's mother clamps her hands over the boy's ears, but he wriggles free.)* What do you think of sex, Colonel Brady?

58

BRADY. In what spirit is this question asked?

DRUMMOND. I'm not asking you what you think of sex as a father, or as a husband. Or a Presidential candidate. You're up here as an expert on the Bible. What's the Biblical evaluation of sex?

BRADY. It is considered "Original Sin."

DRUMMOND. *(With mock amazement.)* And all these holy people got themselves "begat" through "Original Sin"? *(Huge reaction from outraged spectators. Brady does not answer. He scowls and shifts his weight in the chair.)* All this sinning make 'em any less holy?

DAVENPORT. *(Leaping up and speaking through spectator reaction.)* Your Honor, where is this leading us? What does it have to do with the State versus Bertram Cates?

JUDGE. *(Gavels the spectators quiet.)* Colonel Drummond, the court must be satisfied that this line of questioning has some bearing on the case. *(Drummond slams the Bible on the Judge's bench.)*

DRUMMOND. *(Fiery.)* You've ruled out all my witnesses. I must be allowed to examine the one witness you've left me in my own way!

BRADY. *(With dignity.)* Your Honor, I am willing to sit here and endure Mr. Drummond's sneering and his disrespect. For he is pleading the case of the prosecution by his contempt for all that is holy.

DRUMMOND. I object, I object, I object. *(Pounds his table.)*

BRADY. On what grounds? It is possible that something *is* holy to the celebrated agnostic?

DRUMMOND. *Yes! (His voice drops, intensely.)* The individual human mind. In a child's power to master the multiplication table there is more sanctity than in all your shouted "Amens!" "Holy, Holies!" and "Hosannahs!" An idea is a greater monument than a cathedral. And the advance of man's knowledge is more of a miracle than any sticks turned to snakes, or the parting of waters! But are we now to halt the march of progress because Mr. Brady frightens us with fable? *(Crossing to the jury, reasonably.)* Gentlemen, progress has never been a bargain. You've got to pay for it. Sometimes I think there's a man behind a counter who says, "All right, you can have a telephone; but you'll have to give up privacy, the charm of distance. Madam, you may vote; but at a price; you lose the right to retreat behind a powder-puff or a petticoat.

59

(Pointing to the sky.) Mister, you may conquer the air, but the birds will lose their wonder, and the clouds will smell of gasoline!" *(Thoughtfully, seeming to look beyond the courtroom.)* Darwin moved us forward to a hilltop, where we could look back and see the way from which we came. But for this view, this insight, this knowledge, we must abandon our faith in the pleasant poetry of Genesis.

BRADY. We must *not* abandon faith! Faith is the important thing!

DRUMMOND. Then why did God plague us with the power to think? Mr. Brady, why do you deny the *one* faculty which lifts man above all other creatures on the earth: the power of his brain to reason? What other merit have we? The elephant is larger, the horse is stronger and swifter, the butterfly more beautiful, the mosquito more prolific, even the simple sponge is more durable! *(Wheeling on Brady.)* Or does a *sponge* think?

BRADY. I don't know. I'm a man, not a sponge. *(There are a few snickers at this, the crowd seems to be slipping away from Brady and aligning itself more and more with Drummond.)*

DRUMMOND. Do you think a sponge thinks?

BRADY. *(Uncomfortably.)* If the Lord wishes a sponge to think, it thinks.

DRUMMOND. Does a man have the same privileges that a sponge does?

BRADY. Of course.

DRUMMOND. *(Roaring, for the first time: crossing and stretching his arm toward Cates.)* This man wishes to be accorded the same privilege as a sponge! *He wishes to think! (There is applause from the scientists. The sound of it strikes Brady exactly as if he had been slapped in the face. Even the faithful are beginning to doubt the infallibility of their champion.)*

BRADY. But your client is wrong! He is deluded! He has lost his way!

DRUMMOND. It's sad that we aren't all gifted with your positive knowledge of Right and Wrong, Mr. Brady. *(Drummond strides to Dr. Page, and takes from him a rock, about the size of a tennis ball. Drummond weighs the rock in his hand as he saunters back toward Brady.)* How old do you think this rock is? *(Davenport rises, about to object.)*

BRADY. *(Intoning.)* I am more interested in the Rock of Ages, than I am in the Age of Rocks. *(A couple of die-hard "Amens." Drummond ignores this glib gag.)*

DRUMMOND. Dr. Page of Oberlin College tells me that this rock is at least ten million years old. *(Davenport looks to Judge.)*

BRADY. *(Sarcastically.)* Well, well, Colonel Drummond! You managed to sneak in some of that scientific testimony after all. *(Davenport sits. Drummond opens up the rock, which splits into two halves.)*

DRUMMOND. Look, Mr. Brady. These are the fossil remains of a pre-historic marine creature, which was found in this very county — and which lived here millions of years ago, when these very mountain ranges were submerged in water.

BRADY. I know. The Bible gives me a fine account of the flood. But your professor is a little mixed up on his dates. That rock is not more than six thousand years old.

DRUMMOND. How do you know?

BRADY. A fine Biblical scholar, Bishop Usher, has determined for us the exact date and hour of the Creation. It occurred in the Year 4004 B.C.

DRUMMOND. That's Bishop Usher's opinion.

BRADY. It is not an opinion. It is literal fact, which the good Bishop arrived at through careful computation of the ages of the prophets as set down in the Old Testament. In fact, he determined that the Lord began the Creation on the 23rd of October in the Year 4004 B.C. at — uh, 9 A.M.!

DRUMMOND. That Eastern Standard Time? *(Laughter.)* Or Rocky Mountain Time? *(More laughter.)* It wasn't daylight-saving time, was it? Because the Lord didn't make the sun until the fourth day!

BRADY. *(Fidgeting.)* That is correct.

DRUMMOND. *(Sharply.)* That first day. Was it a twenty-four hour day?

BRADY. The Bible says it was a day.

DRUMMOND. There wasn't any sun. How do you know how long it was?

BRADY. *(Determined.)* The Bible says it was a day.

DRUMMOND. A normal day, a literal day, a twenty-four-hour day? *(Pause. Brady is unsure.)*

BRADY. I do not know.

DRUMMOND. What do you think?

BRADY. *(Floundering.)* I do not think about things that ... I do not think about!

DRUMMOND. Do you ever think about things that you *do* think about? *(There is some laughter. But it is dampened by the awareness, throughout the courtroom, that the trap is about to be sprung.)* Isn't it possible that first day was twenty-five hours long? There was no way to measure it, no way to tell! *Could* it have been twenty-five hours? *(Pause. The entire courtroom seems to lean forward.)*

BRADY. *(Hesitates — then.)* It is ... *possible* ... *(Gasp of shock from spectators. Many spring to their feet. Drummond's got him. And he knows it! This is the turning point. From here on, the tempo mounts. Drummond is now fully in the driver's seat. He pounds his questions faster and faster.)*

DRUMMOND. Oh. You interpret that the first day recorded in the Book of Genesis could be of indeterminate length.

BRADY. *(Wriggling.)* I mean to state that the day referred to is not necessarily a twenty-four-hour day.

DRUMMOND. It could have been thirty hours! Or a month! Or a year! Or a hundred years! *(Seizing the rock, he brandishes it underneath Brady's nose.)* Or ten million years! *(Huge reaction of mixed protest and wonder from spectators. Davenport is able to restrain himself no longer. He realizes that Drummond has Brady in his pocket. Red-faced, he leaps up.)*

DAVENPORT. *(Shouting through spectator reaction.)* I protest! This is not only irrelevant, immaterial — it is *illegal!* *(The courtroom is a storm of impassioned, arguing voices. The Judge pounds for order, but the emotional tension will not subside.)* I demand to know the purpose of Mr. Drummond's examination! What is he trying to do?

BRADY. *(Rises from the witness chair.)* I'll tell you what he's trying to do. He wants to destroy everybody's belief in the Bible, and in God!

DRUMMOND. You know that's not true. I'm trying to stop you bigots and ignoramuses from controlling the education of the United States! And you know it! *(Another roar of confusion from spectators, some even join the scientists' applause. Meeker rises in a vain attempt to restore order. Arms out, Davenport pleads to the court, but is unheard. The Judge hammers for order.)*

JUDGE. *(Shouting.)* I shall ask the bailiff to clear the court, unless there is order here.

BRADY. How dare you attack the Bible?

DRUMMOND. The Bible is a book. A good book. But it's not the *only* book.

BRADY. It is the revealed work of the Almighty. God spake to the men who wrote the Bible.

DRUMMOND. And how do you know that God didn't "spake" to Charles Darwin?

BRADY. I know, because God tells me to oppose the evil teachings of that man.

DRUMMOND. Oh, God speaks to *you.*

BRADY. Yes.

DRUMMOND. He tells you exactly what's right and what's wrong?

BRADY. *(Doggedly.)* Yes.

DRUMMOND. And you act accordingly?

BRADY. Yes.

DRUMMOND. So you, Matthew Harrison Brady, through oratory, legislation, or whatever, pass along God's orders to the rest of the world! *(Laughter begins.)* Gentlemen, meet the "Prophet From Nebraska!" *(Brady's oratory is unassailable, but his vanity — exposed by Drummond's prodding — is only funny. The laughter is painful to Brady. He starts to answer Drummond, then turns toward the spectators and tries, almost physically, to suppress the amused reaction. This only makes it worse.)*

BRADY. *(Almost inarticulate.)* I — Please — !

DRUMMOND. *(With increasing tempo, closing in.)* Is that the way of things?

BRADY. No.

DRUMMOND. God tells Brady what is good!

BRADY. No.

DRUMMOND. To be against Brady is to be against God! *(More laughter.)*

BRADY. *(Confused.)* No, no! Each man is a free agent —

DRUMMOND. Then what is Bertram Cates doing in the Hillsboro jail? *(Applause from the scientists and more townspeople.)*

63

Suppose Mr. Cates had enough influence and lung power to railroad through the State Legislature a law that only *Darwin* should be taught in schools!

BRADY. Ridiculous, ridiculous! There is only one great Truth in the world —

DRUMMOND. The Gospel according to Brady! God speaks to Brady, and Brady tells the world! Brady, Brady, Brady, Almighty! *(Drummond bows grandly. The crowd laughs.)*

BRADY. The Lord is my strength —

GOODFELLOW. *(Giggling.)* It is kinda funny.

KREBS. *(Plaintively.)* What's the matter with him?

DRUMMOND. What if a lesser human being — a Cates, or a Darwin — has the audacity to think that God might whisper to *him*? That an un-Brady thought might still be holy? Must men go to prison because they are at odds with the self-appointed prophet? *(Brady is now trembling so that it is impossible for him to speak. He rises, towering above his tormentor — rather like a clumsy, lumbering bear that is baited by an agile dog.)* Extend the Testaments! Let us have a Book of Brady! We shall hex the Pentateuch, and slip you in neatly between Numbers and Deuteronomy! *(The court is in an uproar with arguments and laughter. Brady is almost in a frenzy.)*

BRADY. *(Reaching for a sympathetic ear, trying to find the loyal audience which has slipped away from him.)* My friends — Your Honor — My Followers — Ladies and Gentlemen —

DRUMMOND. The witness is excused. *(Crosses to his chair, gathers his things. Judge rises, gavels violently for order. Meeker crosses to spectators, trying to quiet them.)*

BRADY. All of you know what I stand for! What I believe!

JUDGE. You are excused, Colonel Brady. You are excused, Colonel Brady.

BRADY. I believe, I believe in the truth of the Book of Genesis! *(With both clenched fists he pounds the air, rhythmic hammer-blows of conviction as he fervently recites the books of the Old Testament.)*
Exodus
Leviticus
Numbers

DRUMMOND. Your Honor, this completes my testimony. The witness is excused.

BRADY. *(With mounting fervor, not stopping.)*
Deuteronomy
Joshua
Judges
Ruth
First Samuel —
JUDGE. Court is adjourned till ten o'clock tomorrow morning. *(Gavel. The spectators begin to mill about. A number of them, reporters and curiosity-seekers, cluster around Drummond. Davenport follows the Judge out.)*
DAVENPORT. Your Honor, I want to speak to you about striking all of this from the record. *(They go out. The Jurors, filing out, stare at the strange sight of this man nailing down his faith on the empty air.)*
BRADY. *(Still erect on the witness stand.)*
Second Samuel
First Kings
Second Kings
Isaiah
Jeremiah
Lamentations
Ezekiel
Daniel
Hosea
Joel
Amos
Obadiah —
(Mrs. Brady, nearly in tears, moves toward her husband, looking over her shoulder at the departing Hornbeck, wishing him and all the others gone. Brady continues to beat the air with his clenched fists.)
Jonah
Micah
Nahum
Habakkuk
Zephaniah —
(His voice trails off. His fists seem to turn into putty as he sinks limp and exhausted into the witness chair.)
Haggai

Zechariah

Malachi …

(Mrs. Brady watches Drummond with helpless anger as most of the crowd follow Drummond out of the courtroom. Brady sits, ignored on the witness chair. Mrs. Brady goes to her husband, takes his hand.)

MRS. BRADY. Matt — *(There is distant laughter from offstage. Brady looks about to make sure everyone has left the courtroom before he speaks.)*

BRADY. Mother. They're laughing at me, Mother.

MRS. BRADY. *(Unconvincingly.)* No, Matt. No, they're not!

BRADY. I can't stand it when they laugh at me. *(Mrs. Brady steps up onto the raised level of the witness chair. She stands beside and behind her husband, putting her arms around the massive shoulders and cradling his head against her breast.)*

MRS. BRADY. *(Soothing.)* It's all right, baby. It's all right. *(Mrs. Brady sways gently back and forth, as if rocking a child to sleep.)* Baby … Baby…! *(The lights fade.)*

Scene 2

The courtroom, the following day. The lighting is low, somber. A spot burns down on the defense table, where Drummond and Cates sit, waiting for the jury to return. Drummond leans back in a meditative mood, feet propped on a chair. Cates, the focus of the furor, is resting his head in his arms. The courtroom is almost empty. In comparative shadow, Brady sits, eating a box lunch. He is drowning his troubles with food, as an alcoholic escapes from reality with a straight shot. Hornbeck enters, bows low to Brady, imitating Drummond's bow of mock-obeisance, tips his boater.

HORNBECK. Afternoon, Colonel. Having high tea, I see. *(Brady ignores him.)* Is the jury still out? Swatting flies and wrestling with justice — in that order? *(Brady continues eating,*

ignoring him. Hornbeck crosses to Drummond. Cates lifts his head.)
I'll hate to see the jury filing in; won't you, Colonel? I'll miss
Hillsboro — especially this courthouse: A mélange of Moorish
and Methodist; it must have been designed by a congressman.
*(Hornbeck smirks at his own joke, then lies down on the second row
of spectator chairs and pores over a newspaper. Neither Cates nor
Drummond has paid the slightest attention to him.)*
CATES. *(Staring straight ahead.)* Mr. Drummond. What's going
to happen?
DRUMMOND. What do you think is going to happen, Bert?
CATES. Do you think they'll send me to prison?
DRUMMOND. They could.
CATES. They don't ever let you see anybody from the outside, do
they? I mean — you can't just talk to a visitor — through a window — the way they show in the movies?
DRUMMOND. Oh, it's not as bad as all that. *(Turning toward
the town.)* When they started this fire here, they never figured it
would light up the whole sky. A lot of people's shoes are getting
hot. But you can't be too sure. *(At the other side of the stage, Brady
rises majestically from his debris of paper napkins and banana peels,
and goes off.)*
CATES. *(Watching Brady go.)* He seems so sure. He seems to know
what the verdict's going to be.
DRUMMOND. Nobody knows. *(He tugs on one ear.)* I've got a
pretty good idea. When you've been a lawyer as long as I have —
a thousand years, more or less — you get so you can smell the way
a jury's thinking.
CATES. What are they thinking right now?
DRUMMOND. *(Sighing.)* Some day I'm going to get me an *easy*
case. An open-and-shut case. I've got a friend up in Chicago. Big
lawyer. Lord how the money rolls in! You know why? He never
takes a case unless it's a sure thing. Like a jockey who won't go in
a race unless he can ride the favorite.
CATES. You sure picked the long shot this time, Mr. Drummond.
DRUMMOND. Sometimes I think the law *is* like a horse race.
Sometimes it seems to me I ride like fury, just to end up back where
I started. Might as well be on a merry-go-round, or a rocking horse
... or ... *(He half-closes his eyes. His voice is far away, his lips barely*

move.) Golden Dancer …

CATES. What did you say?

DRUMMOND. That was the name of my first long shot. Golden Dancer. She was in the big side window of the general store in Wakeman, Ohio. I used to stand out in the street and say to myself, "If I had Golden Dancer I'd have everything in the world that I wanted." *(He cocks an eyebrow.)* I was seven years old, and a very fine judge of rocking horses. *(He looks off again into the distance.)* Golden Dancer had a bright red mane, blue eyes, and she was gold all over, with purple spots. When the sun hit her stirrups, she was a dazzling sight to see. But she was a week's wages for my father. So Golden Dancer and I always had a plate glass window between us. *(Reaching back for memory.)* But — let's see, it wasn't Christmas; must've been my birthday — I woke up in the morning and there was Golden Dancer at the foot of my bed! Ma had skimped on the groceries, and my father'd worked nights for a month. *(Re-living the moment.)* I jumped into the saddle and started to rock — *(Almost a whisper.)* And it *broke!* It split in two! The wood was rotten, the whole thing was put together with spit and sealing wax! All shine, and no substance! *(Turning to Cates.)* Bert, whenever you see something bright, shining, perfect-seeming — all gold, with purple spots — look behind the paint! And if it's a lie — show it up for what it really is! *(A Radio Man comes on, lugging an old-fashioned carbon microphone. The Judge, carrying his robe over his arm, comes on and scowls at the microphone.)*

RADIO MAN. *(To Judge.)* I think this is the best place to put it — if it's all right with you, Your Honor.

JUDGE. There's no precedent for this sort of thing.

RADIO MAN. You understand, sir, we're making history here today. This is the first time a public event has ever been broadcast.

JUDGE. Well, I'll allow it — provided you don't interfere with the business of the court.

RADIO MAN. Thank you, sir! *(The Radio Man starts to string his wires. The Mayor hurries on, worried, brandishing a telegram. Radio Man calls to assistant offstage, "Coming, Ed!" And exits.)*

MAYOR. *(To Judge.)* Merle, gotta talk to you. Over here. *(He draws the Judge aside, not wanting to be heard.)* This wire just came. The boys over at the state capitol are getting worried about how things are going. Newspapers all over are raising such a hullaballoo. The boys are beginning to feel nervous. After all, November ain't too far off, and it don't do any of us any good to have any of the voters gettin' all steamed up. Wouldn't do no harm to just let things simmer down. *(The Radio Man reappears. Crosses to his microphone.)* Well, go easy, Merle. *(Tipping his hat to Drummond, the Mayor hurries off.)*

RADIO MAN. *(Crisply, into the mike.)* Testing 1 — 2 — 3 — 4 — 5. *(Judge exits. Drummond rises.)* Testing 1 — 2 — 3 — 4 — 5. *(Drummond crosses to the microphone.)*

DRUMMOND. *(To the Radio Man.)* What's that?

RADIO MAN. An enunciator.

DRUMMOND. You going to broadcast?

RADIO MAN. We have a direct wire to WGN, Chicago. As soon as the jury comes in, we'll announce the verdict. *(Drummond takes a good look at the microphone.)*

DRUMMOND. Radio! God, this is going to break down a lot of walls.

RADIO MAN. *(Hastily.)* You're — you're not supposed to say "God!" on the radio!

DRUMMOND. Why the hell not? *(The Radio Man looks at the microphone, as if it were a toddler that had just been told the facts of life.)*

RADIO MAN. You're not supposed to say "Hell," either.

DRUMMOND. *(Sauntering back to his chair.)* This is going to be a barren source of amusement! *(Brady re-enters and crosses ponderously to the Radio Man.)*

BRADY. Can one speak into either side of this machine? *(The Radio Man starts at this rumbling thunder, so close to the ear of his delicate child.)*

RADIO MAN. *(In an exaggerated whisper.)* Yes, sir. Either side. *(Brady attempts to lower his voice, but it is like putting a leash on an elephant.)*

BRADY. Kindly signal me while I am speaking, if my voice does not have sufficient projection for your radio apparatus. *(Lights bump up to full. A voice offstage is heard yelling loudly, "Jury's comin' back in." Suddenly the air is charged with excitement as the spectators scurry expectantly back to their seats. Meeker enters, crosses to the*

69

Judge's bench, reaches up for the gavel and raps it several times.)
MEEKER. Everybody rise. *(Everybody rises. The Judge enters and sits.)* Hear ye, hear ye. Court will reconvene in the case of the State versus Bertram Cates. *(The court sits. Meeker waves jury on. They enter, faces fixed and stern, and take their seats.)*
CATES. *(As jury files in, whispers to Drummond.)* What do you think? Can you tell from their faces? *(Drummond is nervous, too. He squints at the returning jurors, drumming his fingers on the table top. Cates looks around, as if hoping to see Rachel — but she is not there. His disappointment is evident. The Radio Man has received his signal from offstage, and he begins to speak into the microphone. Spectators are chattering excitedly.)*
RADIO MAN. *(Low, with dramatic intensity.)* Ladies and gentlemen, this is Harry Y. Esterbrook, speaking to you from the courthouse in Hillsboro, where the jury is just returning to the courtroom to render its verdict in the famous Hillsboro Monkey Trial case. The Judge has just taken the bench. And in the next few minutes we shall know whether Bertram Cates will be found innocent or guilty. *(The Judge looks at him with annoyance, waving him to stop. Gingerly the Radio Man aims his microphone at the Judge and steps back. Spectators quiet. There is hushed tension all through the courtroom.)*
JUDGE. *(Clears his throat.)* Gentlemen of the Jury, have you reached a decision?
SILLERS. *(Rising.)* Yeah. Yes, sir, we have, Your Honor. *(Meeker crosses to Sillers and takes a slip of paper from him. Silently, he crosses to the Judge's bench, gives Judge verdict note and crosses to his chair. All eyes following the slip of paper. The Judge takes it, opens it, raps his gavel.)*
JUDGE. The jury's decision is unanimous. Bertram Cates is found guilty as charged! *(There is tremendous reaction. Some cheers, applause, "Amens." Some boos. Brady is pleased. But is not the beaming powerful, assured Brady of the Chautauqua tent. It is a bitter victory for him, not a conquest with a cavalcade of angels. Cates stares at his lap. Drummond taps a pencil. The Radio Man talks rapidly, softly into his microphone. The Judge does not attempt to control the reaction.)*
RADIO MAN. Did you hear that, friends out there in radio land?

Bertram Cates has been found guilty as charged. I can tell you the confusion here is simply unbelievable and now the next voice you hear will be that of the Judge actually pronouncing sentence.

HORNBECK. *(In the manner of a hawker or pitchman.)* Step right up, and get your tickets for the Middle Ages! You only *thought* you missed the Coronation of Charlemagne!

JUDGE. *(Raps his gavel. The noise quiets down.)* The prisoner will rise, to hear the sentence of this court. *(Drummond looks up quizzically, alert.)* Bertram Cates, I hereby sentence you to —

DRUMMOND. *(Sharply.)* Your Honor! *(Rises.)* A question of procedure!

JUDGE. *(Nettled.)* Well, sir?

DRUMMOND. It is not customary in this state to allow the defendant to make a statement before sentence is passed? *(The Judge is red-faced.)*

JUDGE. Colonel Drummond, I regret this omission. In the confusion, and the — I neglected — *(Drummond sits. To Cates.)* Uh, Mr. Cates, if you wish to make any statement before sentence is passed on you, why, you may proceed. *(Clears throat again. Cates rises.)*

CATES. *(Simply.)* Your Honor, I am not a public speaker. I do not have the eloquence of some of the people you have heard in the last few days. I'm just a schoolteacher.

MRS. BLAIR. Not any more you ain't!

CATES. *(Pause. Quietly.)* I *was* a schoolteacher. *(With difficulty.)* I feel I am ... I have been convicted of violating an unjust law. I will continue in the future, as I have in the past, to oppose this law in any way I can. I — *(Cates isn't sure exactly what to say next. He hesitates, then sits down. There is a crack of applause from scientists. Brady is fretful and disturbed. He's won the case. The prize is his, but he can't reach the candy. In his hour of triumph, Brady expected to be swept from the courtroom on the shoulders of his exultant followers. But the drama isn't proceeding according to plan. The gavel again. The court quiets down.)*

JUDGE. Bertram Cates, this court has found you guilty of violating Public Act Volume 37, Statute Number 31428, as charged. This violation is punishable by fine and/or imprisonment. *(He coughs.)* But since there has been no previous violation of this statute, there

71

is no precedent to guide the bench in passing sentence. *(He flashes the automatic smile.)* The court deems it proper — *(He glances at the Mayor.)* to sentence Bertram Cates to pay a fine of — *(He coughs.)* one hundred dollars. *(The mighty Evolution Law explodes with the pale puff of a wet firecracker. There is a murmur of surprise through the courtroom. Brady is indignant. He rises, incredulous.)*

BRADY. Did your honor say one hundred dollars?

JUDGE. That is correct. *(Trying to get it over with.)* This seems to conclude the business of the trial —

BRADY. *(Thundering.)* Your Honor, the prosecution takes exception! Where the issues are so titanic, the court must mete out more drastic punishment —

DRUMMOND. *(Biting in. Rising.)* I object!

BRADY. To make an example of this transgressor! To show the world —

DRUMMOND. Just a minute. Just a minute. The amount of the fine is of no concern for me. Bertram Cates has no intention whatsoever of paying this or any other fine.

MRS. BLAIR. Let him go to jail then.

DRUMMOND. He would not pay it if it were one single dollar. We will appeal this decision to the Supreme court of this state. Will the court grant thirty days to prepare our appeal?

JUDGE. Granted. The court fixes bond at … five hundred dollars. I believe this concludes the business of this trial. Therefore, I declare this court is adjour —

BRADY. *(Hastily.)* Your Honor! *(He reaches for a thick manuscript.)* Your Honor, with the court's permission, I should like to read into the record a few short remarks which I have prepared —

DRUMMOND. *(Rises.)* I object to that. Mr. Brady may make any remarks he likes — long, short or otherwise. In a Chautauqua tent or in a political campaign. Our business in Hillsboro is completed. The defense holds that the court shall be adjourned.

BRADY. *(Frustrated.)* But I have a few remarks —

JUDGE. And we are all anxious to hear them, sir. But Colonel Drummond's point of procedure is well taken. I am sure that everyone here will wish to remain after the court is adjourned to hear your address. *(Drummond sits. Brady lowers his head slightly, in gracious deference to procedure. The Judge raps the gavel.)* I hereby

declare this court is adjourned, sine die. *(Everybody rises except Drummond and Cates. There is a babble of confusion and reaction. Hornbeck promptly crosses to Meeker and confers with him in whispers. Hawker with ice cream box of Eskimo Pies shouts loudly.)*
HAWKER. Eskimo Pies. Get your Eskimo Pies! *(Judge raps with his gavel.)*
JUDGE. *(Projecting.)* Quiet! Order in the — I mean, your attention, please. *(The court quiets.)* We are honored to hear a few words from Colonel Brady, who wishes to address you — *(The Judge is interrupted in his introduction by Meeker and Hornbeck. They confer sotto voce. The babble of voices crescendos.)*
HAWKER. Get your Eskimo Pies! Cool off with an Eskimo Pie! *(Howard and Melinda cross to Radio Man and annoy him. Davenport and Brown help Brady mount his chair. Brady preens himself for the speech, but is annoyed by the confusion. Hornbeck hands the Judge several bills from his wallet, and Meeker pencils a receipt. The Judge bangs the gavel again.)*
JUDGE. We beg your attention, please, ladies and gentlemen! Colonel Brady has some remarks to make which I am sure will interest us all. *(Brady stretches out his arms, in the great attention-getting gesture.)*
BRADY. My dear friends...! Your attention, please! *(The bugle voice reduces the noise somewhat. But it is not the eager, anticipatory hush of olden days. Attention is given him, not as the inevitable due of a mighty monarch, but grudgingly and resentfully.)* Fellow citizens, and friends of the unseen audience. From the hallowed hills of sacred Sinai, in the days of remote antiquity, came the law which has been our bulwark and our shield. Age upon age, men have looked to the law as they would look to the mountains, whence cometh our strength. And here, here in this — *(The Radio Man approaches Brady nervously.)*
RADIO MAN. Excuse me, Mr. — uh, Colonel Brady — would you ... uh ... step a little closer to the enunciator...?
BRADY. *(Indicating Davenport's chair.)* Here?
RADIO MAN. Fine. *(Brady, helped by Radio Man steps to Davenport chair. Radio Man crosses back to his microphone. In this momentary lull, the audience has slipped away from him again. Even Mrs. Brady, trying to quiet people, is turned away from her*

husband. Brady's vanity and cussedness won't let him give up, even though he realizes this is a sputtering anticlimax. By God, he'll make them listen. Simultaneously.)

BRADY. *(Red-faced, his larynx taut, roaring stridently.)* As they would look to the mountains whence cometh our strength. And here, here in this courtroom, we have seen vindicated — *(A few people leave. He watches them desperately, out of the corner of his eye.)* We have seen vindicated —

RADIO MAN. *(After an offstage signal.)* Ladies and gentlemen, our program director in Chicago advises us that our time here is completed. Harry Y. Esterbrook speaking. We return you now to our studios and "Matinee Musicale." *(Radio Man takes the microphone and goes off. This is the final indignity to Brady, he realizes that a great portion of his audience has left him. Brady brandishes his speech, as if it were Excalibur. His eyes start from his head, the voice is a tight, frantic rasp.)*

BRADY. From the hallowed hills of sacred Sinai ... *(He freezes. His lips move, but nothing comes out. Paradoxically, his silence brings silence. The orator can hold his audience only by not speaking.)*

GOODFELLOW. Look at him!

MRS. BRADY. *(Spinning around, with terror.)* Matt — *(There seems to be some violent, volcanic upheaval within him. His lower lip quivers, his eyes stare. Very slowly, he seems to be leaning toward the audience. Then, like a figure in a waxworks, toppling from its pedestal, he falls stiffly, face forward. Meeker and Davenport spring forward, catch Brady by the shoulders and break his fall. The sheaf of manuscript, clutched in his raised hand, scatters in mid air. The great words flutter innocuously to the courtroom floor. There is a burst of reaction. Mrs. Brady screams.)*

DAVENPORT. Get a doctor! *(Mrs. Brady rushes to his side.)*

MRS. BRADY. Matt! Dear God in Heaven! Matt! *(Drummond, Hornbeck and Cates watch, silent and concerned. Mrs. McLain dashes to Brady, kneels.)*

MRS. McLAIN. *(Wailing.)* O Lord, work us a miracle and save our Holy Prophet! *(Rudely, Meeker pushes her back.)*

MEEKER. *(Contemptuously.)* Get away. *(Crisply.)* Move him out of here. Fast as we can. George. Bill. Give us a hand here. Get him across the street to Doc's office. *(Sillers and several other men lift Brady, with difficulty, and begin to carry him out. A strange thing happens. Brady, his head tilted downstage, begins to speak in a hollow, distant voice — as if something sealed up inside of him were finally broken, and the precious contents spilled out into the open at last.)*

BRADY. *(As he is carried out, in a strange, unreal voice.)* Mr. Chief Justice, Citizens of these United States. During my term in the White House, I pledge to carry out my program for the betterment of the common people of this country. *(Brady is off.)* As your new President, I say what I have said all of my life ... *(The crowd tags along, curious and awed. Only Drummond, Cates and Hornbeck remain, their eyes fixed on Brady's exit.)*

DRUMMOND. How quickly they can turn. And how painful it can be when you don't expect it. *(He turns.)* I wonder how it feels to be Almost-President three times — with a skull full of undelivered inauguration speeches.

HORNBECK. Something happens to an Also-Ran. Something happens to the feet of a man who always comes in second in a foot-race. He becomes a national unloved child, a balding orphan, an aging adolescent who never got the biggest piece of candy. Show me a shouter and I'll show you an Also-Ran. A might-have-been. An almost-was.

CATES. *(Softly.)* Did you see his face? He looked terrible ... *(Meeker enters. Cates turns to him. Meeker shakes his head: "I don't know.")*

MEEKER. I'm surprised more folks ain't keeled over in this heat. *(He picks up Brady's speech from the floor.)*

HORNBECK. He's all right. Give him an hour or so to sweat away the pickles and the pumpernickel; to let his tongue forget the acid taste of vinegar victory. Mount Brady will erupt again by nightfall, *(Picks up a page from Brady's speech and reads.)* spouting lukewarm fire and irrelevant ashes. *(Cates shakes his head, bewildered. Drummond watches him, concerned.)*

DRUMMOND. What's the matter, boy?

CATES. I'm not sure. Did I win or did I lose?

DRUMMOND. You won.

CATES. But the jury found me —

DRUMMOND. What jury? Twelve men? Millions of people will

say you won. They'll read in their papers tonight that you smashed a bad law. You made it a joke!

CATES. Yeah. But what's going to happen now? I haven't got a job. I'll bet they won't even let me back in the boarding house.

DRUMMOND. Sure, it's gonna be tough, it's not gonna be any church social for a while. But you'll live. And while they're making you sweat, remember — you've helped the next fella.

CATES. What do you mean?

DRUMMOND. You don't suppose this kind of thing is ever finished, do you? Tomorrow, sure as hell, somebody else'll have to stand up. And you've helped give him the guts to do it!

CATES. *(Turning to Meeker, with new pride in what he's done.)* Mr. Meeker, don't you have to lock me up?

MEEKER. They fixed bail.

CATES. You don't expect a schoolteacher to have five hundred dollars.

MEEKER. *(Jerking his head toward Hornbeck.)* This fella here put up the money.

HORNBECK. *(With a magnanimous gesture.)* With a year's subscription to the Baltimore *Herald*, we give away — at no cost or obligation — a year of freedom. *(Rachel enters, carrying a suitcase. There is a new lift to her head. Cates turns to see her.)*

CATES. Rachel!

RACHEL. Hello, Bert.

CATES. *(Indicating her suitcase.)* I don't need any more shirts. I'm free — for a while anyway.

RACHEL. These are *my* things, Bert. I'm going away.

CATES. Where are you going?

RACHEL. I'm not sure. But I'm leaving my father.

CATES. Rache …

RACHEL. Bert, it's my fault the jury found you guilty. *(He starts to protest.)* Partly my fault. I helped. *(Rachel hands Bert the orange book.)* This is your book, Bert. *(Silently, he takes it.)* I've read it. All the way through. I don't understand it. What I do understand, I don't like. I don't want to think that men come from apes and monkeys. But I think that's beside the point. *(Drummond looks at the girl admiringly.)*

DRUMMOND. That's right. That's beside the point. *(Rachel*

crosses to Drummond.)

RACHEL. Mr. Drummond, I hope I haven't said anything to offend you. *(He shakes his head.)* You see, I haven't really thought very much. I was always afraid of what I might think — so it seemed safer not to think at all. But now I know. A thought is like a child inside our body. It has to be born. If it dies inside you, part of you dies, too! *(Pointing to the book.)* Maybe what Mr. Darwin wrote is bad. I don't know. Bad or good, it doesn't make any difference. The ideas have to come out — like children. Some of 'em healthy as a bean plant, some sickly. I think the sickly ideas die mostly, don't you, Bert? *(Bert nods yes, but he's too lost in new admiration for her to do anything but stare. He does not move to her side. Drummond smiles, as if to say: "That's quite a girl!" The Judge walks in slowly.)*

JUDGE. *(Quietly.)* Brady's dead. *(They all react.)*

DRUMMOND. I can't imagine the world without Matthew Harrison Brady.

CATES. What caused it? Did they say? *(Dazed, the Judge goes off without answering.)*

HORNBECK. Matthew Harrison Brady died of a busted belly. *(Drummond slams down his brief case.)* Be frank! Why should we weep for him? He cried enough for himself! The national tear duct from Weeping Water, Nebraska, who flooded the whole nation like a one-man Mississippi! You know what he was: a Barnum-bunkum Bible-beating bastard! *(Drummond rises, fiercely angry.)*

DRUMMOND. You smart-aleck! You have no more right to spit on his religion than you have a right to spit on *my* religion! Or my lack of it!

HORNBECK. *(Askance.)* Well, what do you know! Henry Drummond for the defense — even of his enemies!

DRUMMOND. *(Low, moved.)* There was much greatness in this man.

HORNBECK. Shall I put that in the obituary? *(Drummond starts to pack up his brief case.)*

DRUMMOND. Write anything you damn please.

HORNBECK. How do you write an obituary for a man who's been dead thirty years? "In Memoriam — M.H.B." Then what? Hail the apostle whose letters to the Corinthians were lost in the mail? Ten years, *two* years — and tourists will ask the guide, "Who died there? Matthew Harrison Who?" *(A sudden thought.)* What did he say to the minister? It fits! He delivered his own obituary! *(Hornbeck crosses to Judge's bench, finds the Bible.)* Here it is: his book! *(Thumbing hastily.)* Proverbs, wasn't it?

DRUMMOND. *(Quietly.)* "He that troubleth his own house shall inherit the wind: *(Turns to Hornbeck.)* and the fool shall be servant to the wise in heart." *(Hornbeck looks at Drummond, surprised. He snaps the Bible shut, and lays it on the bench. Hornbeck folds his arms and crosses slowly toward Drummond, his eyes narrowing.)*

HORNBECK. Well, well, Colonel Drummond! We're growing an odd crop of agnostics this year!

DRUMMOND. *(Evenly.)* I'm getting damned tired of you, Hornbeck.

HORNBECK. Why?

DRUMMOND. You never pushed a noun against a verb except to blow up something.

HORNBECK. That's a typical lawyer's trick: accusing the accuser!

DRUMMOND. What am I accused of?

HORNBECK. I charge you with contempt of conscience! Self perjury. Kindness aforethought! Sentimentality in the first degree.

DRUMMOND. Why? Because I refuse to erase a man's lifetime? I tell you Brady had the same rights as Cates: the right to be wrong!

HORNBECK. "Be-Kind-To-Bigots" Week. Since Brady's dead, we must be kind. God, how the world is rotten with kindness!

DRUMMOND. A giant once lived in that body. *(Quietly.)* But Matt Brady got lost. Because he was looking for God too high up and too far away.

HORNBECK. You hypocrite! You fraud! *(With a growing sense of discovery.)* You're more religious than *he* was! *(Drummond doesn't answer.)* Excuse me, gentlemen. I must get me to a typewriter and hammer out the story of an atheist — who believes in God! *(He slaps his straw hat on his head and goes off.)*

CATES. Colonel Drummond.

DRUMMOND. Bert, I am resigning my commission in the State Militia. I hand in my sword!

CATES. Doesn't it cost a lot of money for an appeal? I couldn't pay you ... *(Drummond waves him off.)*

DRUMMOND. I didn't come here to be paid. *(Putting on his hat.)* Well, I'd better get myself on a train.

RACHEL. There's one out at five-thirteen. Bert, you and I can be on that train, too!

CATES. *(Smiling, happy.)* I'll get my stuff!

RACHEL. I'll help you! *(They start off. Rachel remembers her suitcase, runs back for it. Cates grabs his suit jacket, clasps Drummond's arm.)*

CATES. *(Calling over his shoulder.)* See you at the depot! *(Rachel and Cates go off. Drummond is left alone on stage. Suddenly he notices Rachel's copy of Darwin on the table, picks it up and calls off.)*

DRUMMOND. Say — you forgot — *(But Rachel and Cates are out of earshot. He rotates the volume in his hand, this one book has been the center of the whirlwind. Then he looks at the book, decides to take it with him. He is about to put it into his brief case when he notices the Bible, at the edge of the Judge's bench. His brief case tucked under his arm, the orange Darwin in one hand, he crosses to the bench, picks up the Bible in his other hand. He holds them both in his upturned palms, stares from one volume to the other, balancing them thoughtfully, as if his hands were scales, and they teeter with equal weight. He half-smiles, half-shrugs. Drummond resoundingly slaps the books together — SIDE BY SIDE — then jams them into his brief case, neither one on top. Slowly, he climbs to the level of the empty town square, leaving as he has arrived, alone, off to fight another battle.)*

Curtain

FURNITURE AND PROPERTY PLOT

Pre-set at courtroom level:
Judge's bench and high-backed leather chair.
Witness chair, dark mahogany with arms, set on 6" high platform.
Platform should have at least 10" lip at front end.
2 counsel tables (19" wide, 40" long)
4 straight-backed counsel chairs, dark mahogany
Thin reporters' table, several scarred straight-backed chairs.
Small table and stool for Meeker (Left of Judge's bench)
Stool for Court Reporter (Right of Judge's bench)
21 court-room chairs, straight-backed, for spectators and scientists.

In Dry Goods Store window:
2 suits, suspenders; 4 hats

In Drug Store window:
Apothecary jars with colored liquid; suspended glass globes with colored liquid, dimly lit during night-time scenes.

To be carried on:
Picnic table (18" wide, 38" long)
Portable platform (for prayer meeting)
Two folding-chairs (for platform)

Hand-props:
Multi-colored, hand-printed signs, each mounted on a stick or pole, in sharp-bold letters, reading:
    ARE YOU A MAN OR A MONKEY?
    AMEND THE CONSTITUTION — PROHIBIT DARWIN
    SAVE OUR SCHOOLS FROM SIN
    MY ANCESTORS AIN'T APES!
    WELCOME, MATTHEW HARRISON BRADY
    DOWN WITH DARWIN
    BE A SWEET ANGEL
    DON'T MONKEY WITH OUR SCHOOLS!
    DARWIN IS WRONG!
    DOWN WITH EVOLUTION

DO YOU WANT WINGS OR HORNS?
DARWIN IS THE DEVIL
BAR DARWIN!
MY UNCLE AIN'T A MONKEY
Hot dog wagon (or box) with 3 hot dogs in rolls and wax paper
Eskimo pie box
Eskimo pies (in box)
Old-fashioned microphone on stand with wire (marked: WGN)
Large platter of fried chicken parts (not eaten).
Large bowl of potato salad, small bowl containing two or three
apricots, large bowl of fruit salad, paper plates, napkins, silverware,
large serving spoons in all bowls.
Water glass one-half filled with water (for Judge's table)
Brief case (DAVENPORT)
Gladstone bag braced to support actor when set on end
(HORNBECK)
Push broom (MEEKER)
Hand towel (MEEKER)
Hammer (DUNLAP)
Screwdriver (SILLERS)
Fountain pen (MEEKER)
Shaving cream (MEEKER)
Folded newspaper copy-paper (HORNBECK)
Tear sheet (HORNBECK)
Steno pad (COURT RECORDER)
Pencil
Shoe box containing sandwich, cookies, napkins (BRADY)
Baltimore newspaper (HORNBECK)
Paper money (HORNBECK)
Gavel
Large law book
Court Bible
Roster of jurymen
Revival note
2 indictments
Note pad
Receipt pad
Apple (HORNBECK)

Handkerchief — large (MRS. BRADY)
Brief case with indictments and legal papers (DRUMMOND)
Brady speech
Verdict note (SILLERS)
Darwin book (bright orange)
Watch (MEEKER)
Watch (RADIO MAN)
Folder of legal papers (JUDGE)
Hurdy gurdy and live monkey (ORGAN GRINDER)
Bass drum — harness — and stick
"Read Your Bible" canvas or cloth banner
Halyards and pulleys for raising banner
Lemonade stand set with pitcher, spoon, sign, paper cups
Small suitcase (RACHEL)
Shirt, tie, handkerchief (in small suitcase)
Trumpet (BOLLINGER)
Cloth shopping bag with fans (MRS. McLAIN)
Old type bellows camera (PHOTOGRAPHER)
Box with fossil rock (DR. ALLEN PAGE)
Note pads (REPORTERS)
Pencils (REPORTERS)
Watch (REV. BROWN)
Watch (DRUMMOND)
Mayor's speech (MAYOR)
Honorary Colonel certificate (MAYOR)
Box with Bibles (ELIJAH)
Telegram (MAYOR)
Suitcase (DRUMMOND)
Tin can (HOWARD)
Improvised fishing pole (HOWARD)
Worms (pre-set on the Courthouse lawn)
Paper plate with one-half eaten drumstick, dab of potato salad and fork (for Brady switch)

COSTUME PLOT

HENRY DRUMMOND: Light brown suit, blue and white striped shirt, white collar, broad lavender suspenders, dark blue tie, black hat, black shoes.

MATTHEW HARRISON BRADY: Black coat, grey striped trousers, light tan pongee shirt, high black shoes, black bow tie, Panama hat.

E.K. HORNBECK: Two piece grey tweed suit, light blue shirt, hard straw hat, dark blue tie, black shoes.

JUDGE: Two piece black alpaca suit, black robe, white shirt, black four-in-hand tie, black shoes.

REV. BROWN: Two piece black suit, white shirt, black string tie, black shoes.

BERTRAM CATES: Tan trousers, light blue-grey shirt, brown shoes. Then: Two piece brown suit, white shirt, bow tie, brown shoes.

RACHEL: Yellow crepe blouse, tan linen skirt, black pumps. Later: Blue crepe dress and matching belt, black pumps. Final scene: Green cotton blouse, green linen skirt and jacket, black pumps.

MRS. BRADY: White cotton blouse, two piece white linen suit, off white straw hat, white shoes, white crocheted string gloves, white crocheted pocketbook, white taffeta parasol, white hose.

MRS. BLAIR: Blue and white figured crepe dress, white shoes, string of white beads, black shoes.

MRS. KREBS: Black figured voile dress, black bag, black shoes.

MRS. McLAIN: Lavender and white figured cotton dress, black flat shoes.

MELINDA: White cotton blouse, red and white cotton jumper, black shoes (Mary Janes), white anklet socks. Then: Peach sateen dress, black shoes (Mary Janes), white anklet socks.

MRS. LOOMIS: Lavender checked cotton jumper, lavender cotton blouse, black shoes.

MAYOR'S WIFE: Tan chiffon dress, light tan straw hat with violets, cream lace handbag, brown shoes.

DAVENPORT: Two piece white suit, tan shirt, tan tie, white shoes.

MAYOR: Two piece white suit, striped cotton shirt, brown striped tie, brown shoes, hard straw hat.

HOWARD: Tan knickers, tan shirt, blue sneakers, brown knee length socks. Later: Tan suit jacket, tan knickers, tan shirt, blue sneakers, bow tie.

SILLERS: Grey trousers, white shirt, black work shoes. Later: Two piece grey suit, blue striped shirt, brown tie, black shoes, sleeve garters.

JESSE H. DUNLAP: Dark blue jacket, black trousers, brown striped shirt, black tie, black shoes.

GOODFELLOW: Brown and white seersucker suit, tan and white striped shirt, striped bow tie, suspenders, hard straw hat, brown shoes.

PHOTOGRAPHER — RADIO MAN: PHOTOGRAPHER: Brown striped trousers, cream silk shirt without collar, grey vest, hard straw hat, black work shoes. RADIO MAN: Dark grey two piece suit, white shirt, black tie, black shoes.

COOPER — REUTERS MAN: COOPER: Black suit jacket, grey trousers, white shirt, black shoes. REUTERS MAN: Two piece brown and green tweed suit, light blue shirt, tan knit tie, tan and cream oxfords.

MEEKER: Black trousers, white collarless shirt, suspenders, black shoes. Then: Two piece black suit, white shirt, black tie, black shoes.

ORGAN GRINDER: Brown corduroy trousers, plaid shirt, dark blue vest, soft felt hat.

BOLLINGER: Grey and white seersucker trousers, tan shirt without collar, suspenders, black work shoes.

BANNISTER: Grey suit jacket, black trousers, white shirt, brown tie. Black shoes.

FINNEY — HOT DOG MAN — DRUMMER — ESKIMO PIE MAN: HOT DOG MAN: Light tan trousers, white shirt, white cap. DRUMMER: Light tan trousers, white shirt, white cap. FINNEY: Dark brown trousers, dark grey suit coat, grey vest, bow tie, suspenders, black shoes, white shirt.

ELIJAH: Dark grey trousers, white shirt, black vest.

PHIL — COURT RECORDER: PHIL: Olive green trousers, white shirt, black shoes. COURT RECORDER: Olive green trousers, white shirt, bow tie, black suit jacket, black shoes.

TIMMY: Light grey trousers, white shirt, white sneakers.

DR. AMOS D. KELLER: Two piece grey suit, white shirt, brown knit tie, brown shoes.

DR. ALLEN PAGE: Two piece light blue suit, white shirt, maroon tie, black shoes.

WALTER AARONSON: Two piece light brown suit, white shirt, bow tie, brown shoes.

DOC KIMBLE: Three piece dark grey suit, white shirt, bow tie, black shoes.

JURORS: Wear trousers, shirts, some with ties, some with vests. All wear suit jackets, not necessarily matching with pants.

3 REPORTERS: Wear regular suits better in cut than the townspeople's clothes.

PRODUCTION NOTES BY THE PLAYWRIGHTS

INHERIT THE WIND is not about the theory of evolution versus the literal interpretation of the Bible. It assaults those who would constrict any human being's right to think, to teach, to learn. Our major theme is "the dignity of the individual human mind."

The play has been translated and produced in 34 languages. It is most effective when performed on two levels, with no pause except at the act-break, and with a near-cinematic flow between the town square and the courtroom. Humanity is on trial. Anyone who would limit thought is on trial.

These must be utterly believable people, shorn of any trace of caricature. Avoid the use of Southern accents; they tend to make the play seem sectional rather than universal. Your program should read:

The Place: A small town.

The Time: Not too long ago.

MATTHEW HARRISON BRADY begins as a giant, filled with charisma and confidence, beloved of the people. Then, as in a Greek tragedy, we watch him fall, topple from his pedestal. He must not be a "paper-tiger," his vulnerability telegraphed in advance. But he should be a dynamic figure of power and substance, three times nearly President. For his warm and sunlit entrance, pound that drum, sound that trumpet. In contrast, the tinkling of the hurdy-gurdy will give an effective entrance for the maverick HENRY DRUMMOND, the loner, making his unheralded arrival into the almost-empty town square, a looming solo shadow projected by the hot red sunset.

RACHEL BROWN charts the parabola of the play as her mind travels the difficult journey from innocent compliance to a more-embracing capacity to receive new thoughts, new ideas. She relives the terror of her childhood as if it were happening then and now. Later, an unwilling witness, she becomes mute, trapped as her emotions battle between genuine love of Bert Cates and duty to her Father. When she explains her growing enlightenment in the final scene, she gropes for self-understanding, mystified, bewildered by what seems to be going on inside her, like a mother sensing the first heart-beat of her unborn child.

BERT CATES, in his confrontation with Rachel in the opening scene, re-dramatizes the moment he was impelled, as a

86

responsible school-teacher to open the book and read it to his class. Bert longs to rush into his girl's arms, but his inquiring spirit is at war with her still-closed mind. He is no martyr; Bert Cates is an intellectual explorer, who vividly relives the moments when his imagination traveled beyond the dark-side of the moon. His statement after sentencing is eloquent, spoken with modest and unaffected simplicity.

REV. JEREMIAH BROWN will be more frightening when he calls down hell-fire on Cates if he appears to be a benevolent pastor in the opening sequences. There is logic and warmth in his approach to his people, but his prayer meeting nearly gets out of hand in its dedicated passion.

E.K. HORNBECK is not a Greek chorus, nor the voice of the playwrights. But he loves to "dance with words," relishing his own turn-of-phrase and sometimes outrageous alliteration. His lines were written originally in blank verse, to match his delight at the rhythm and poetry of language, to illustrate his impudent Pan-like cry at human follies and his feeling that mere prose is simply flat. He uses his folded-newspaper-copy-paper to jot down his own witticisms to print later in his newspaper column, such as his designation of Hillsboro as "the buckle on the Bible Belt," or his observation that the local Courthouse is "A combination of Moorish and Methodist; it must have been designed by a congressman." His boater straw-hat is an inspired prop; he tips it impertinently, uses it to wave away his disdain for the "unplumbed and plumbingless depths" or to point with derision at a new-found target. He brandishes his boater with the panache of a cynical Cyrano. Whereas DRUMMOND takes the high road at play's end to start up a mountain peak of respect-even-for-one's-enemies, HORNBECK keeps traveling the lower road of denigration.

A live monkey and a real hurdy-gurdy will add enormously to the color and excitement, and will heighten HORNBECK'S initial humor. There is much laughter in this play, particularly in the puncturing of inflexibility and pomposity, in the agile thrust-and-parry of DRUMMOND's incisive mind. Be sure DRUMMOND refers to actual passages in the Bible, as he leafs through it during the scene with BRADY on the witness stand.

An alternative method of production would move the judge's bench, jury-box, tables and spectators' chairs on two wagons which could join from either side as the action blends from exterior to interior, without pause. Make certain that the town is always visible, part of the play, part of the trial. (However, your production will be far more effective and fluid if the scenery has no moving parts.)

Arena stage producers will be interested to know that the play had its initial production in theatre-in-the-round at the Margo Jones Theatre in Dallas. The Jury became part of the audience, seating themselves on the arena steps. The prayer-meeting, conducted from dead center, was especially effective in terms of audience involvement, since the celebrants seemed to emerge from all sides, as if from the audience itself. A later arena production (George Keathley directing Luther Adler and Larry Gates at Philadelphia's Playhouse-in-the-Park) placed the witness-chair on a swivel, with DRUMMOND, like an intellectual tiger, circling his prey ready to pounce. The increasingly bated BRADY whirls to find his accuser confronting him from every angle.

Be certain BRADY pounds the air with double fists, rhythmically incanting the names of the books of the Old Testament. The most eloquent line in the play is unspoken: DRUMMOND's weighing of the books at the end. He should be holding them in his upturned palms, balancing them like the scales of Lady Justice, then SLAPPING them together — SIDE BY SIDE. Don't put either Darwin or the Bible on top. *Origin of the Species* should be a distinctive bright orange or green and the book Rachel brings in during the final scene should be identical to the one used by Drummond throughout the trail.

Every performance of this play should feel like an opening night, happening NOW, on your stage for the first time, pertinent to this hour and this day. Each juror, each spectator should have his or her own occupation, distinctive personality, convictions, passions, prejudices, open or closed mind, rate of enlightenment or resistance to change. All are swept into the maelstrom of thought and feeling, of momentous moments as-they-are-happening.

Jerome Lawrence
Robert E. Lee
1986

"INHERIT THE WIND"

ACT II – SCENE I

MUSIC FOR
(ELIJAH'S RESPONSES IN PRAYER MEETING)

And the eve - nin', and the mor - nin' -were the { first } day.
{second}

The Lord made Man mas-ter of the Earth..!

*The music for most of the other hymns can
be found in a variety of standard hymnals*

89

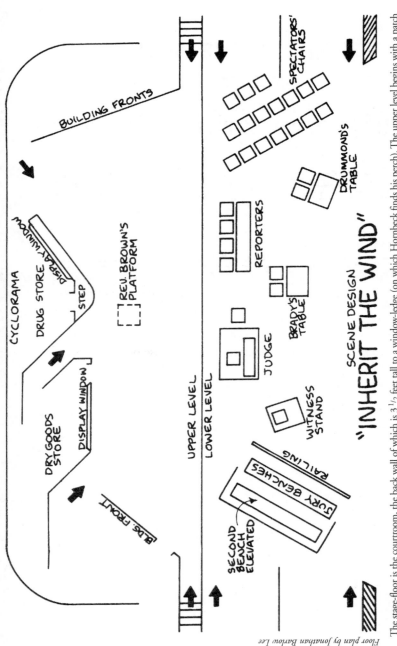

CYCLORAMA

BUILDING FRONTS

DRUG STORE

DISPLAY WINDOW

STEP

DRY GOODS STORE

DISPLAY WINDOW

BLDG. FRONT

REV. BROWN'S PLATFORM

UPPER LEVEL

LOWER LEVEL

JUDGE

WITNESS STAND

BRADY'S TABLE

REPORTERS

DRUMMOND'S TABLE

SPECTATORS' CHAIRS

JURY BENCHES

RAILING

SECOND BENCH ELEVATED

SCENE DESIGN

"INHERIT THE WIND"

The stage-floor is the courtroom, the back wall of which is 3 1/2 feet tall to a window-ledge (on which Hornbeck finds his perch). The upper level begins with a patch of courthouse lawn, raking gradually upstage toward the converging entrances of the town-square. No scenic element moves on or off except for the portable platform which is brought on à vista for the prayer meeting. As stated in the stage directions, "the town is visible always, as much on trial as the individual defendant."

AFTERWORD

Lawrence and Lee's *Inherit the Wind* remains strikingly relevant more than fifty years after its first performance. It has been translated into more than thirty languages, and has enjoyed literally thousands of productions, major revivals, and film and television adaptations.

Since *Inherit the Wind* first roused audiences at Margo Jones' theatre in Dallas — and subsequently opened on Broadway in April 1955 — the controversy over the teaching of evolution in the public schools has only intensified. How astonished Jerry Lawrence and Bob Lee would be by this fact.

They wrote *Inherit* as a response to McCarthyism, but they also saw the play as a very personal testament to their belief in the compatibility of faith and reason. Bob was raised a Methodist in the small town of Elyria, Ohio; Jerry, born just a few miles away in Cleveland, was raised in a deeply observant Jewish household. Over their lifetimes, they each sustained an abiding faith in God and religious principles. Bob wrote, "Religion means a great deal to me. But Jesus did not burden the disciples with creeds and credos. He said: 'Follow me.' More important than observing any formal ritual is the ethical result of the religious experience. Religion urges us to use our intuition of the divine in our practical, hour-to-hour tasks of working and living."

Protesting the action of the Rockford, Illinois School Board, which had sought to cancel a 1963 high school production of *Inherit*, the playwrights wrote, "We feel that *Inherit the Wind* is entirely in accord with a basic religious tenet: each man his own priest."

Both Lawrence and Lee felt that the religious experience is essentially mystical — and very different for every individual. They did not intend *Inherit the Wind* to be perceived as an attack on fundamentalism, nor as a battle between science and religion. They wrote, "Ministers of many faiths have preached sermons about this play because they believe, as we do, that educated, scientifically aware people may still believe, deeply, in God."

Mrs. Robert E. Lee
Encino, California
January 2009

NEW PLAYS

★ **MOTHERS AND SONS by Terrence McNally.** At turns funny and powerful, MOTHERS AND SONS portrays a woman who pays an unexpected visit to the New York apartment of her late son's partner, who is now married to another man and has a young son. Challenged to face how society has changed around her, generations collide as she revisits the past and begins to see the life her son might have led. "A resonant elegy for a ravaged generation." –NY Times. "A moving reflection on a changed America." –Chicago Tribune. [2M, 1W, 1 boy] ISBN: 978-0-8222-3183-7

★ **THE HEIR APPARENT by David Ives, adapted from Le Légataire Universel by Jean-François Regnard.** Paris, 1708. Eraste, a worthy though penniless young man, is in love with the fair Isabelle, but her forbidding mother, Madame Argante, will only let the two marry if Eraste can show he will inherit the estate of his rich but miserly Uncle Geronte. Unfortunately, old Geronte has also fallen for the fair Isabelle, and plans to marry her this very day and leave her everything in his will—separating the two young lovers forever. Eraste's wily servant Crispin jumps in, getting a couple of meddling relatives disinherited by impersonating them (one, a brash American, the other a French female country cousin)—only to have the old man kick off before his will is made! In a brilliant stroke, Crispin then impersonates the old man, dictating a will favorable to his master (and Crispin himself, of course)—only to find that rich Uncle Geronte isn't dead at all and is more than ever ready to marry Isabelle! The multiple strands of the plot are unraveled to great comic effect in the streaming rhyming couplets of French classical comedy, and everyone lives happily, and richly, ever after. [4M, 3W] ISBN: 978-0-8222-2808-0

★ **HANDLE WITH CARE by Jason Odell Williams.** Circumstances both hilarious and tragic bring together a young Israeli woman, who has little command of English, and a young American man, who has little command of romance. Is their inevitable love an accident…or is it destiny, generations in the making? "A hilarious and heart-warming romantic comedy." –NY Times. "Hilariously funny! Utterly charming, fearlessly adorable and a tiny bit magical." –Naples News. [2M, 2W] ISBN: 978-0-8222-3138-7

★ **LAST GAS by John Cariani.** Nat Paradis is a Red Sox-loving part-time dad who manages Paradis' Last Convenient Store, the last convenient place to get gas—or anything—before the Canadian border to the north and the North Maine Woods to the west. When an old flame returns to town, Nat gets a chance to rekindle a romance he gave up on years ago. But sparks fly as he's forced to choose between new love and old. "Peppered with poignant characters [and] sharp writing." –Portland Phoenix. "Very funny and surprisingly thought-provoking." –Portland Press Herald. [4M, 3W] ISBN: 978-0-8222-3232-2

DRAMATISTS PLAY SERVICE, INC.
440 Park Avenue South, New York, NY 10016 212-683-8960 Fax 212-213-1539
postmaster@dramatists.com www.dramatists.com

NEW PLAYS

★ **ACT ONE by James Lapine.** Growing up in an impoverished Bronx family and forced to drop out of school at age thirteen, Moss Hart dreamed of joining the glamorous world of the theater. Hart's famous memoir *Act One* plots his unlikely collaboration with the legendary playwright George S. Kaufman and his arrival on Broadway. Tony Award-winning writer and director James Lapine has adapted Act One for the stage, creating a funny, heartbreaking and suspenseful celebration of a playwright and his work. "…brims contagiously with the ineffable, irrational and irrefutable passion for that endangered religion called the Theater." –NY Times. "…wrought with abundant skill and empathy." –Time Out. [8M, 4W] ISBN: 978-0-8222-3217-9

★ **THE VEIL by Conor McPherson.** May 1822, rural Ireland. The defrocked Reverend Berkeley arrives at the crumbling former glory of Mount Prospect House to accompany a young woman to England. Seventeen-year-old Hannah is to be married off to a marquis in order to resolve the debts of her mother's estate. However, compelled by the strange voices that haunt his beautiful young charge and a fascination with the psychic current that pervades the house, Berkeley proposes a séance, the consequences of which are catastrophic. "…an effective mixture of dark comedy and suspense." –Telegraph (London). "A cracking fireside tale of haunting and decay." –Times (London). [3M, 5W] ISBN: 978-0-8222-3313-8

★ **AN OCTOROON by Branden Jacobs-Jenkins. Winner of the 2014 OBIE Award for Best New American Play.** Judge Peyton is dead and his plantation Terrebonne is in financial ruins. Peyton's handsome nephew George arrives as heir apparent and quickly falls in love with Zoe, a beautiful octoroon. But the evil overseer M'Closky has other plans—for both Terrebonne and Zoe. In 1859, a famous Irishman wrote this play about slavery in America. Now an American tries to write his own. "AN OCTOROON invites us to laugh loudly and easily at how naïve the old stereotypes now seem, until nothing seems funny at all." –NY Times [10M, 5W] ISBN: 978-0-8222-3226-1

★ **IVANOV translated and adapted by Curt Columbus.** In this fascinating early work by Anton Chekhov, we see the union of humor and pathos that would become his trademark. A restless man, Nicholai Ivanov struggles to dig himself out of debt and out of provincial boredom. When the local doctor, Lvov, informs Ivanov that his wife Anna is dying and accuses him of worsening her condition with his foul moods, Ivanov is sent into a downward spiral of depression and ennui. He soon finds himself drawn to a beautiful young woman, Sasha, full of hope and energy. Finding himself stuck between a romantic young mistress and his ailing wife, Ivanov falls deeper into crisis, heading toward inevitable tragedy. [8M, 8W] ISBN: 978-0-8222-3155-4

DRAMATISTS PLAY SERVICE, INC.
440 Park Avenue South, New York, NY 10016 212-683-8960 Fax 212-213-1539
postmaster@dramatists.com www.dramatists.com

NEW PLAYS

★ **I'LL EAT YOU LAST: A CHAT WITH SUE MENGERS by John Logan.** For more than 20 years, Sue Mengers' clients were the biggest names in show business: Barbra Streisand, Faye Dunaway, Burt Reynolds, Ali MacGraw, Gene Hackman, Cher, Candice Bergen, Ryan O'Neal, Nick Nolte, Mike Nichols, Gore Vidal, Bob Fosse…If her clients were the talk of the town, she was the town, and her dinner parties were the envy of Hollywood. Now, you're invited into her glamorous Beverly Hills home for an evening of dish, dirty secrets and all the inside showbiz details only Sue can tell you. "A delectable soufflé of a solo show…thanks to the buoyant, witty writing of Mr. Logan" –NY Times. "80 irresistible minutes of primo tinseltown dish from a certified master chef." –Hollywood Reporter. [1W] ISBN: 978-0-8222-3079-3

★ **PUNK ROCK by Simon Stephens.** In a private school outside of Manchester, England, a group of highly-articulate seventeen-year-olds flirt and posture their way through the day while preparing for their A-Level mock exams. With hormones raging and minimal adult supervision, the students must prepare for their future — and survive the savagery of high school. Inspired by playwright Simon Stephens' own experiences as a teacher, PUNK ROCK is an honest and unnerving chronicle of contemporary adolescence. "[A] tender, ferocious and frightning play." –NY Times. "[A] muscular little play that starts out funny and ferocious then reveals its compassion by degrees." –Hollywood Reporter. [5M, 3W] ISBN: 978-0-8222-3288-9

★ **THE COUNTRY HOUSE by Donald Margulies.** A brood of famous and longing-to-be-famous creative artists have gathered at their summer home during the Williamstown Theatre Festival. When the weekend takes an unexpected turn, everyone is forced to improvise, inciting a series of simmering jealousies, romantic outbursts, and passionate soul-searching. Both witty and compelling, THE COUNTRY HOUSE provides a piercing look at a family of performers coming to terms with the roles they play in each other's lives. "A valentine to the artists of the stage." –NY Times. "Remarkably candid and funny." –Variety. [3M, 3W] ISBN: 978-0-8222-3274-2

★ **OUR LADY OF KIBEHO by Katori Hall.** Based on real events, OUR LADY OF KIBEHO is an exploration of faith, doubt, and the power and consequences of both. In 1981, a village girl in Rwanda claims to see the Virgin Mary. Ostracized by her schoolmates and labeled disturbed, everyone refuses to believe, until impossible happenings appear again and again. Skepticism gives way to fear, and then to belief, causing upheaval in the school community and beyond. "Transfixing." –NY Times. "Hall's passionate play renews belief in what theater can do." –Time Out [7M, 8W, 1 boy] ISBN: 978-0-8222-3301-5

DRAMATISTS PLAY SERVICE, INC.
440 Park Avenue South, New York, NY 10016 212-683-8960 Fax 212-213-1539
postmaster@dramatists.com www.dramatists.com

NEW PLAYS

★ **AGES OF THE MOON by Sam Shepard.** Byron and Ames are old friends, reunited by mutual desperation. Over bourbon on ice, they sit, reflect and bicker until fifty years of love, friendship and rivalry are put to the test at the barrel of a gun. "A poignant and honest continuation of themes that have always been present in the work of one of this country's most important dramatists, here reconsidered in the light and shadow of time passed." –NY Times. "Finely wrought…as enjoyable and enlightening as a night spent stargazing." –Talkin' Broadway. [2M] ISBN: 978-0-8222-2462-4

★ **ALL THE WAY by Robert Schenkkan. Winner of the 2014 Tony Award for Best Play.** November, 1963. An assassin's bullet catapults Lyndon Baines Johnson into the presidency. A Shakespearean figure of towering ambition and appetite, this charismatic, conflicted Texan hurls himself into the passage of the Civil Rights Act—a tinderbox issue emblematic of a divided America—even as he campaigns for re-election in his own right, and the recognition he so desperately wants. In Pulitzer Prize and Tony Award–winning Robert Schenkkan's vivid dramatization of LBJ's first year in office, means versus ends plays out on the precipice of modern America. ALL THE WAY is a searing, enthralling exploration of the morality of power. It's not personal, it's just politics. "…action-packed, thoroughly gripping… jaw-dropping political drama." –Variety. "A theatrical coup…nonstop action. The suspense of a first-class thriller." –NY1. [17M, 3W] ISBN: 978-0-8222-3181-3

★ **CHOIR BOY by Tarell Alvin McCraney.** The Charles R. Drew Prep School for Boys is dedicated to the creation of strong, ethical black men. Pharus wants nothing more than to take his rightful place as leader of the school's legendary gospel choir. Can he find his way inside the hallowed halls of this institution if he sings in his own key? "[An] affecting and honest portrait…of a gay youth tentatively beginning to find the courage to let the truth about himself become known." –NY Times. "In his stirring and stylishly told drama, Tarell Alvin McCraney cannily explores race and sexuality and the graces and gravity of history." –NY Daily News. [7M] ISBN: 978-0-8222-3116-5

★ **THE ELECTRIC BABY by Stefanie Zadravec.** When Helen causes a car accident that kills a young man, a group of fractured souls cross paths and connect around a mysterious dying baby who glows like the moon. Folk tales and folklore weave throughout this magical story of sad endings, strange beginnings and the unlikely people that get you from one place to the next. "The imperceptible magic that pervades human existence and the power of myth to assuage sorrow are invoked by the playwright as she entwines the lives of strangers in THE ELECTRIC BABY, a touching drama." –NY Times. "As dazzling as the dialogue is dreamful." –Pittsburgh City Paper. [3M, 3W] ISBN: 978-0-8222-3011-3

DRAMATISTS PLAY SERVICE, INC.
440 Park Avenue South, New York, NY 10016 212-683-8960 Fax 212-213-1539
postmaster@dramatists.com www.dramatists.com